LETTERS FROM THE QUEEN OF NAVARRE
WITH AN *AMPLE DECLARATION*

The Other Voice in Early Modern Europe:
The Toronto Series, 43

MEDIEVAL AND RENAISSANCE
TEXTS AND STUDIES

VOLUME 490

T0385737

The Other Voice in
Early Modern Europe:
The Toronto Series

SERIES EDITORS Margaret L. King *and* Albert Rabil, Jr.
SERIES EDITOR, ENGLISH TEXTS Elizabeth H. Hageman

Previous Publications in the Series

The Other Voice in Early Modern Europe: The Toronto Series

SERIES EDITORS Margaret L. King *and* Albert Rabil, Jr.
SERIES EDITOR, ENGLISH TEXTS Elizabeth H. Hageman

Previous Publications in the Series

The Other Voice in
Early Modern Europe:
The Toronto Series

SERIES EDITORS Margaret L. King *and* Albert Rabil, Jr.
SERIES EDITOR, ENGLISH TEXTS Elizabeth H. Hageman

Previous Publications in the Series

The Other Voice in
Early Modern Europe:
The Toronto Series

SERIES EDITORS Margaret L. King *and* Albert Rabil, Jr.
SERIES EDITOR, ENGLISH TEXTS Elizabeth H. Hageman

Previous Publications in the Series

JEANNE FLORE
Tales and Trials of Love, Concerning Venus's Punishment of Those Who Scorn True Love and Denounce Cupid's Sovereignity: A Bilingual Edition and Study
Edited and translated by Kelly Digby Peebles
Poems translated by Marta Rijn Finch
Volume 33, 2014

VERONICA GAMBARA
Complete Poems: A Bilingual Edition
Critical introduction by Molly M. Martin
Edited and translated by Molly M. Martin and Paola Ugolini
Volume 34, 2014

CATHERINE DE MÉDICIS AND OTHERS
Portraits of the Queen Mother: Polemics, Panegyrics, Letters
Translation and study by Leah L. Chang and Katherine Kong
Volume 35, 2014

FRANÇOISE PASCAL, MARIE CATHERINE DESJARDINS, ANTOINETTE DESHOULIÈRES, AND CATHERINE DURAND
Challenges to Traditional Authority: Plays by French Women Authors, 1650–1700
Edited and translated by Perry Gethner
Volume 36, 2015

FRANCISZKA URSZULA RADZIWIŁŁOWA
Selected Drama and Verse
Edited by Patrick John Corness and Barbara Judkowiak
Translated by Patrick John Corness
Translation Editor Aldona Zwierzyńska-Coldicott
Introduction by Barbara Judkowiak
Volume 37, 2015

DIODATA MALVASIA
Writings on the Sisters of San Luca and Their Miraculous Madonna
Edited and translated by Danielle Callegari and Shannon McHugh
Volume 38, 2015

MARGARET VAN NOORT
Spiritual Writings of Sister Margaret of the Mother of God (1635–1643)
Edited by Cordula van Wyhe
Translated by Susan M. Smith
Volume 39, 2015

GIOVAN FRANCESCO STRAPAROLA
The Pleasant Nights
Edited and translated by Suzanne Magnanini
Volume 40, 2015

The Other Voice in
Early Modern Europe:
The Toronto Series

SERIES EDITORS Margaret L. King *and* Albert Rabil, Jr.
SERIES EDITOR, ENGLISH TEXTS Elizabeth H. Hageman

Previous Publications in the Series

ANGÉLIQUE DE SAINT-JEAN ARNAULD
D'ANDILLY
Writings of Resistance
Edited and translated by John J. Conley, S.J.
Volume 41, 2015

FRANCESCO BARBARO
The Wealth of Wives: A Fifteenth-Century Marriage Manual
Edited and translated by Margaret L. King
Volume 42, 2015

JEANNE D'ALBRET

Letters from the Queen of Navarre
with an *Ample Declaration*

~

Edited and translated by
KATHLEEN M. LLEWELLYN, EMILY E. THOMPSON,
AND COLETTE H. WINN

Iter Academic Press
Toronto, Ontario

Arizona Center for Medieval and Renaissance Studies
Tempe, Arizona

2016

Iter Academic Press
Tel: 416/978–7074   Email: iter@utoronto.ca
Fax: 416/978–1668   Web: www.itergateway.org

Arizona Center for Medieval and Renaissance Studies
Tel: 480/965–5900   Email: mrts@acmrs.org
Fax: 480/965–1681   Web: acmrs.org

Library of Congress Cataloging-in-Publication Data

Names: Jeanne d'Albret, Queen of Navarre, 1528–1572, author. | Llewellyn, Kathleen M., editor and translator. | Thompson, Emily E., editor and translator. | Winn, Colette H., editor and translator. | Jeanne d'Albret, Queen of Navarre, 1528–1572. Ample déclaration.

Title: Jeanne d'Albret : letters from the Queen of Navarre with an ample declaration / edited and translated by Kathleen M. Llewellyn, Emily E. Thompson, and Collette H. Winn.

Other titles: Correspondence. English. | Ample déclaration.

Description: Tempe, Arizona : Arizona Center for Medieval and Renaissance Studies ; Toronto, Ontario : Iter Academic Press, [2016] | Series: The other voice in early modern Europe ; 43 | Series: Medieval and renaissance texts and studies ; volume 490 | Includes bibliographical references and index.

Identifiers: LCCN 2015042129 (print) | LCCN 2015047111 (ebook) | ISBN 9780866985451 (pbk. : alk. paper) | ISBN 9780866987172 ()

Subjects: LCSH: Jeanne d'Albret, Queen of Navarre, 1528–1572.--Correspondence | Queens--France--Correspondence. | France--Kings and rulers--Correspondence. | France--History--Charles IX, 1560-1574--Sources.

Classification: LCC DC112.J4 A3 2016 (print) | LCC DC112.J4 (ebook) | DDC 944/.028092--dc23

LC record available at http://lccn.loc.gov/2015042129

Cover illustration:
Portrait de Jeanne d'Albret. Bibliothèque nationale de France.

Cover design:
Maureen Morin, Information Technology Services, University of Toronto Libraries.

Typesetting and production:
Iter Academic Press.

Contents

Acknowledgments

This volume is the result of a network of collaboration that goes well beyond the listed names. We thank in particular Dan Nickolai for creating a map of Jeanne's territories, Marian Rothstein for sharing her work and her ideas on Jeanne d'Albret, Carla Zecher for facilitating our access to relevant documents in the Newberry collection and Margaret King for supporting our project and editing our work so meticulously.

Introduction

In the sixteenth century, several European women played critical roles on the public stage. Foremost among these were Elizabeth I, queen of England (1558–1603) and Catherine de' Medici, queen consort (1547–1559) of King Henri II of France and later regent (1560–1563) for her young son, King Charles IX. Jeanne d'Albret, regnant queen of Navarre (1555–1572), may claim a place beside these women rulers. She identified with them through several shared experiences, presenting herself in a letter to Elizabeth I as one of "the nurturing Queens of His Church" (169) and reminding Catherine of a commonality that happened to be crucial to their exercise of power: "since then I have shared in the afflictions of widowhood" (162).[1] Moreover, like Elizabeth and Catherine, Jeanne was actively involved in the tumultuous events of the day. The circumstances of Jeanne's life, and the religious and political upheaval of the end of the sixteenth century, prompted her to write the *Ample Declaration* to justify her remarkable decision, in 1568, to join the forces defending the Protestant stronghold of La Rochelle. This unique text reveals how an exceptional woman understood and defined her political, familial and religious leadership.

A Woman of Strength and Power

From the moment of her birth on November 16, 1528, Jeanne d'Albret lived an extraordinary life. She was born into royalty: her father, Henri II d'Albret (1503–1555) was king of Navarre, and her mother, Marguerite de Valois-Angoulême (1492–1549), also known as Marguerite de Navarre, was the sister of François I, king of France. Jeanne was destined to be queen of Navarre and became one of the leaders of the French Protestants.

Jeanne was exposed to reformist thinking from her early years. Although Marguerite de Navarre remained Catholic all her life, she was deeply influenced by the new religious ideas circulating in France on the eve of what would eventually be called the Reformation. Marguerite's religious beliefs were shaped by the reformist cleric Guillaume Briçonnet, Bishop of Meaux, and the evangelical humanist Jacques Lefèvre d'Étaples. She encouraged reform within the Catholic Church and supported vernacular translations of sacred works. She also vehemently defended and protected a number of persecuted reformists.[2]

---

1. References to the *Ample Declaration* refer to our translation, based on the version included in the compilation, *Histoire de nostre temps, contenant un receuil des choses memorables passées et publiées pour le faict de la religion et estat de la France depuis l'edict de pacification du 23 jour de mars, jusqu'au present*, ed. Christophe Landré and Charles Martel (La Rochelle: [Barthelemy Berton], 1570).

2. For a study of the Reformist leanings of Marguerite de Navarre, see Patricia F. Cholakian and Rouben C. Cholakian, *Marguerite de Navarre: Mother of the Renaissance* (New York: Columbia University

Jeanne's early years were spent in the Norman countryside, not often in her mother's company. However, Marguerite, who had received an exceptional education herself, provided one for her daughter as well.[3] Jeanne's health was always frail, but from childhood her spirit was vigorous and independent. Her will was so exceptionally strong, in fact, that she defied her parents and the king of France, François I, when they attempted to use her as a political pawn. When Jeanne was twelve years old François arranged a marriage between Jeanne and Guillaume de La Marck, duc de Clèves. The marriage was negotiated for political expediency, to buttress diplomatic relations between France and the Duchy of Clèves in the Rhine Valley. In an extraordinary gesture of defiance, Jeanne signed a *protestation* against the marriage. Despite Jeanne's objections—she had to be physically carried to the altar—the marriage was celebrated on June 14, 1541. Due to the bride's young age, the marriage was not consummated. Then, in 1543, the duc de Clèves betrayed François I when he renounced his alliance with France and entered into an alliance with Charles I of Spain. This betrayal so angered the French king that he sent a request to the Pope Paul III to annul the marriage. An annulment was obtained in 1545 on the grounds that the marriage had never been consummated and that it had taken place against Jeanne's protestations.

In 1548, Jeanne married Antoine de Bourbon, duc de Vendôme (1518–1562), head of the house of Bourbon. This marriage, too, was politically motivated, intended by Henri II, then king of France, to consolidate territories in the north and south of France. But this time Jeanne was delighted with her bridegroom because he was handsome, charming, and the first Prince of the Blood, by reason of his descent from King Louis IX. It was evidently a happy marriage for a time. Their son Henri (the future Henri IV of France) was born December 13, 1553, and their daughter, Catherine de Bourbon, was born February 7, 1559. The couple's first two sons died very young, as did a daughter.

Jeanne's father died in 1555, six years after her mother. Jeanne, then twenty-seven, succeeded him as queen of Navarre, Béarn, Basse-Navarre, and numerous fiefs of Guyenne. Jeanne argued forcefully and successfully to have her husband named joint sovereign, and Antoine was designated king of Navarre *jure uxoris* (by right of his wife).

One of the few early modern European women who were rulers in their own name, Jeanne was an effective and respected queen of her territories. She maintained a regular correspondence with two of these female rulers: Elizabeth I and

---

Press, 2006), 171–83.

3. Nancy Lyman Roelker maintains that "There is no doubt that Marguerite's daughter was given an education designed to implement the humanist ideal, that is, the development of both character and intellect through absorption of the classic writings which were the models for the Renaissance." Roelker, *Queen of Navarre, Jeanne d'Albret, 1528–1572* (Cambridge, MA: Belknap Press of Harvard University Press, 1968), 32.

Catherine de' Medici. Three of Catherine's sons were successively king of France: François II (1559–1560), Charles IX (1560–1574), and Henri III (1574–1589). Catherine exercised such power during their reigns, sometimes as regent, other times as advisor, that the period has been called "the age of Catherine de' Medici." Jeanne's own family included two strong women who also exercised significant political power. Louise de Savoie, mother of François I, served as the Regent of France in 1515, 1525–1526, and 1529, during periods of François's absence. Marguerite de Navarre, sister of François I and Jeanne's own mother, helped negotiate the Treaty of Cambrai, known as the Paix des Dames (the Ladies' Peace) between France and the Habsburg Holy Roman Empire. François, who was being held prisoner in Madrid, was released as a condition of this treaty.

Jeanne and the Reformation

By the 1550s, Martin Luther, who had launched the Protestant Reformation in Europe, was already dead. John Calvin, a Frenchman by birth, had established a Protestant center in Geneva where he welcomed Huguenot refugees and trained Calvinist ministers. He maintained a regular correspondence with several leading noblemen and women in the French reformed movement. In 1557, pressed by evangelical noblemen in his territories, Jeanne's husband Antoine de Bourbon brought the Calvinist minister François Le Gay, Sieur de Boisnormand, from Geneva to Navarre, where he subsequently organized a number of Protestant churches. Three years later, Calvin sent Théodore de Bèze (1519–1605), his disciple and ultimately his successor, to Nérac, where the court of Navarre was residing. Bèze's initial mission was to obtain Antoine's commitment to the Reform. He did not succeed in this, for Antoine does not appear to have possessed any consistent religious conviction; the king of Navarre vacillated between Catholicism and the Reformed faith, apparently depending upon which seemed politically expedient at the time. However, during the three months that Bèze preached at their court in Nérac, he forged a close friendship with Jeanne. According to David Bryson, Bèze "did succeed in gaining Jeanne's devoted trust, and remained her mentor and respected 'father' until her death."[4]

Jeanne's religious evolution was independent of that of her husband. It is difficult to trace the path of her conversion, judicious as she was about revealing herself because of perceived threats from France, Spain, and the Vatican. Whatever her initial motivations may have been, on Christmas 1560 she publicly renounced Catholicism and devoted the rest of her life to the advancement of the Reformed church.

---

4. David Bryson, *Queen Jeanne and the Promised Land: Dynasty, Homeland, Religion and Violence in Sixteenth-Century France* (Leiden: Brill, 1999), 111.

On the death in 1560 of the sixteen-year-old French king, François II, his ten-year-old brother Charles IX succeeded, but was too young to govern. Although Antoine sought the regency as first prince of the blood, Charles's mother, Catherine de' Medici, claimed the role of regent and Antoine was forced to settle for the position of lieutenant général of France.[5]

By this time the Reformation was gaining strength in France, particularly among nobles, and Calvin regarded Jeanne as the principal force for the advancement of the Reform in Béarn, Navarre, and Guyenne. In 1563 she decreed the Reformed church to be the official church in Béarn. While it is recognized today that many early modern European women participated in and advanced Protestant movements,[6] it was primarily high-ranking noblewomen who helped institutionalize Protestant reforms, and Jeanne was a prominent member of that small but powerful elite. Kirsi Stjerna remarks that "What is most striking in assessing her contribution to the Reformation is the particular effort [Jeanne] put into instilling the Reformation in her lands through legislation and institutional changes, as much as through sponsoring theological work."[7]

Jeanne worked tirelessly to allow and encourage the spread of the Reformed church in Guyenne. This resulted in her being accused and at times treated as a heretic, a spy, and a traitor to the crown by the Catholic Church. Pope Pius IV threatened her with excommunication in August 1563, and in September of that year, accused her of heresy and ordered her to appear in Rome before a tribunal. She was warned that if she did not appear for this examination, her property would be confiscated and "her lands would be forfeited to the first Catholic prince who could conquer them."[8]

The once happy marriage between Jeanne and Antoine had deteriorated over the years, not least because of Jeanne's adherence to and support of the Reformed church. In one particularly divisive episode, Jeanne was strongly criticized for not restraining or punishing the members of the Reformed church responsible for the iconoclastic violence that occurred in Vendôme in May 1562. Antoine was duc de Vendôme and the tombs of his ancestors were pillaged during this incident. Earlier in 1562, Antoine had installed their son at the French court, where he was raised and educated alongside the French royalty. Jeanne claimed

---

5. For more on the political and gender complexities of this situation see Katherine Crawford, *Perilous Performances: Gender and Regency in Early Modern Europe* (Cambridge, MA: Harvard University Press, 2004).

6. See Merry Wiesner-Hanks, "Protestant Movements," in *The Ashgate Research Companion to Women and Gender in Early Modern Europe*, ed. Allyson M. Polska, Jane Couchman, and Katherine A. McIver (Aldershot, UK: Ashgate, 2013), 129–48.

7. Kirsi Stjerna, *Women and the Reformation* (Malden, MA: Blackwell, 2009), 166.

8. Roland H. Bainton, *Women of the Reformation in France and England* (Minneapolis, MN: Augsburg Publishing House, 1973), 61.

that Antoine forced her to leave Paris and return to Pau, and leave her son behind. For the next five years, Henri was brought up under the supervision of Catherine de' Medici, to be used as a pawn like many royal children of the era, including his own mother, in the political and religious machinations of those in power. Antoine, meanwhile, was mortally wounded during the First War of Religion[9] while fighting on the Catholic side at the siege of Rouen, and died in November 1562. It was not, however, until 1567, after five years apart, that Jeanne was able to recover her son and bring him back to Navarre.

Until 1568, Jeanne favored peaceful measures of reform and tolerance for both Catholic and Protestant worship in her lands as well as a political neutrality that protected the French interests of her son. But when the Third War of Religion[10] broke out in August of that year, she could no longer concern herself solely with her own domains.

Shifting Alliances

The year 1568 marked a profound change in Jeanne d'Albret's personal trajectory. It proved more significant in her life than either 1560 when she openly declared her Reformed faith or 1563 when she began to establish Calvinism in Béarn and Navarre. Examining history from this specific vantage point both provides a historical context for the *Ample Declaration* and aids readers in understanding the precise situation that motivated Jeanne to leave for La Rochelle, join Louis de Condé[11] and Gaspard de Coligny[12] in a civil war, and write.

Jeanne had inherited vast, rich lands from her parents. From her father's side, the kingdom of Navarre and the independent viscounty of Béarn were lands where the Salic Law was not applied and women could thus succeed to the throne. This gave Jeanne full sovereign power over these territories. Through her husband Antoine de Bourbon, Jeanne kept her father's lucrative governorship of Guyenne in the family. Upon Antoine's death, Charles IX respected the hereditary title and granted it to Jeanne's son Henri, only nine years old at the time. The combination of territories and hereditary honors constituted a strong economic base for

9. The first of a series of civil, religious wars in France between 1562 and 1598. The First War of Religion lasted from 1562 until 1563.

10. The Third War of Religion (1568–1570).

11. Louis de Bourbon (1530–1569), prince de Condé, son of Charles de Bourbon, duc de Vendôme, and Françoise d'Alençon, younger brother of Antoine de Bourbon and Jeanne's brother-in-law. He was general in Henri II's army and military leader of the Huguenots in the first decade of France's Wars of Religion. He was suspected to have been involved in the 1560 Conspiracy of Amboise. He was killed at the battle of Jarnac in 1569.

12. Gaspard II de Coligny (1519–1572), Protestant leader, nominated Amiral of France in 1552. His assassination on August 22, 1572 was immediately followed by the Saint Bartholomew's Day Massacre in Paris.

Jeanne and her children, and provided them with significant military potential. Their annual income compared favorably with those of the wealthiest nobles in France.[13] Furthermore, the regional authority of Jeanne and her son put at her disposal a network of people who had traditionally served the Albrets for personal, geographic, economic and political reasons, people who might be counted on for defense and support in the future.[14]

The 1560s revealed, however, just how fragile these advantages were. Although her young son, Henri, was officially governor and lieutenant général of Guyenne as his grandfather and father had been, he was still a minor and held the titles in name only. Charles IX appointed as the king's lieutenant in Haute-Guyenne Blaise de Monluc, whose repression of Protestants and the open antagonism he displayed toward Jeanne clearly undermined Henri's titular authority. Jeanne repeatedly asked the king and queen mother to remove Monluc, but to no avail. Her request in 1568 that Henri assume an active role in supervising Guyenne before he reached majority was flatly refused. So despite the Albret's traditional control over Guyenne, the king of France had effectively intervened to acquire more direct control over this religiously divided region.

In 1567 and 1568, royal interference in Jeanne's sovereign lands, too, was worsening, as Charles IX protected nobles in Béarn and Navarre who rebelled against her, possibly even coaxing their rebellion. Alarmed by the official establishment of Protestantism and encouraged perhaps by the perceived weakness of a widowed queen with a young son, they challenged her political authority by organizing a revolt against Jeanne that prevented her from collecting the income from her lands. Even when Jeanne managed to restore peace, she was pressured by Charles IX to pardon the rebel leaders who thereby remained a threat to her.[15]

If the privileges derived from her father's family were undermined by the French king's interests, local rebellion, and the Pope's threat to declare her a heretic, Jeanne could still rely on her late husband's family to build a power base. After Antoine de Bourbon's death in 1562, Jeanne did not remarry, but rather deliberately cultivated her ties to the Bourbons. This was a useful alliance for Jeanne to exploit because the Bourbon brothers were princes of the blood. Like Jeanne, they were descendants of Louis IX, but unlike her, as men, they stood in

---

13. S. Amanda Eurich, *The Economics of Power: The Private Finances of the House of Foix-Navarre-Albret during the Religious Wars* (Kirksville, MO: Sixteenth Century Journal Publishers, 1994), xiii.

14. For an excellent discussion of the complex clientage system in early modern France, see Sharon Kettering, "Clientage during the French Wars of Religion," *The Sixteenth Century Journal* 20, no. 2 (1989): 221–39, "Patronage and Kinship in Early Modern France," *French Historical Studies* 16, no. 2 (1989): 408–35 and "The Patronage Power of Early Modern French Noblewomen," *The Historical Journal* 32, no. 4 (1989): 817–41, as well as J. Russell Major, "Vertical Ties through Time," *French Historical Studies* 17, no. 4 (1992): 863–71.

15. See *Ample Declaration*, 201.

line for the throne of France. Her son Henri's rank and future prospects in France depended on his Bourbon identity.

Of the surviving members of this family, Jeanne chose to link herself most closely to Louis, Prince de Condé, the lay head of the family after Antoine's death and, along with Amiral Coligny, the leader of the Protestant movement in France. Jeanne strengthened ties to the Prince de Condé by evoking his role as uncle, and father surrogate, to her son Henri. The result of this decision, however, meant that Jeanne would share in all of Condé's fortunes—good and bad. Vying for power at court, Condé and the Guise brothers saw Catherine de' Medici and her young sons as political pawns. Several attempts were made by both camps over the years to isolate the royal family and thus control them better. Implicated in the Tumult of Amboise[16] in 1560 and accused of treason, Condé was nearly executed. The duc de Guise was more successful in 1562 when he "escorted" Catherine and Charles IX from Fontainebleau to his strong-hold of Paris where he was already revered as a military and religious hero. The failure of Condé's attempt in September 1567 to kidnap the king and the queen mother at Meaux—an event known as the "Surprise de Meaux"—triggered the Second War of Religion.[17] The resulting resentment on the part of the king and the queen mother toward Condé inescapably led to a loss of favor for Jeanne as well. In August 1568, fearing retribution, Condé took refuge in La Rochelle and prepared once more for war.

Jeanne had a complex and multilayered relationship with the French royal family. Her overlapping genealogy and the adjacency of her lands to France had long guaranteed Jeanne a certain respect from the royal family. Catherine de' Medici maintained a close relationship with her through the First War of Religion, needing Jeanne as a buffer between France and Spain and as a respected Protestant leader to counterbalance the power of the Catholic Guise family at court. As long as Catherine and Charles IX pursued a policy of compromise between the religious partisans in France, Jeanne held a position of strength.

Many historians, however, see Condé's brazen Surprise de Meaux as a turning point in Catherine and Charles's attitude towards the French Protestants. Certainly their strategy towards Protestant nobles changed noticeably in November 1567 with the loss of the Connétable de Montmorency.[18] This member

---

16. The Tumult of Amboise, also referred to as the Amboise Conspiracy, was a failed attempt chiefly by minor Protestant nobles to kidnap François II at Amboise in March 1560 in order to remove him from the influence of his close advisors and in-laws, the Guise family. The conspiracy was uncovered beforehand and most of the participants were executed. The degree of Condé's involvement was contested then and is still a matter of historical debate today.

17. The Second War of Religion (1567–1568).

18. Anne de Montmorency (1493–1567), military leader, statesman, diplomat, named grand maître de France in 1526 and connétable de France in 1538.

of the Triumvirate,[19] though staunchly Catholic, had also been a mediating figure between the Bourbon and the Guise families before he was fatally wounded in the battle of Saint-Denis.[20] The king's brother Henri (the future Henri III), friendly with the Guise faction at the time, replaced Montmorency as commander of the French forces. Another indication of the hardening position towards the Protestants was the king's dismissal from his council in June 1568 of the Chancellor Michel de l'Hôpital who incarnated the moderate position of the Politiques.[21] At this point, Jeanne's best prospect for retaining any kind of political power and independence was to join forces with Condé and his network of support and trumpet the unjustly denied rights of the Bourbon princes of the blood.

Challenges and Opportunities

Jeanne needed a strong ally, for she had a particularly dangerous enemy: Philip II, the King of Spain.[22] It was this powerful, neighboring monarch who in 1563 had pressured the Pope to excommunicate Jeanne and nullify her rights to govern Navarre. At that time, Catherine and Charles IX had intervened and defended Jeanne, but in 1568 Jeanne could no longer count on their support. Since 1566, Philip had engaged in a brutal repression of Protestants who were challenging his authority in the Netherlands. Jeanne's Navarre, sharing a border with Spain through the contested lands of Upper Navarre and sheltering a burgeoning Protestant state, became increasingly intolerable for Philip. She could expect only constant menace from the south and needed to seek a more secure base from which to exercise her sovereign power and fortify the Protestant cause.

The city of La Rochelle promised Jeanne this security as well as greater political agency in France's unfolding affairs. The strategic city had been taken over by its own Protestant-controlled municipal council in January 1568 and was in that same year conceded to the Protestants by Charles IX in the Edict of Longjumeau. As a fortified city in a Protestant-influenced area of France and moreover boasting a port allowing communication and trade with the Netherlands and England, La Rochelle offered Jeanne a safe refuge from which war could be successfully waged.

---

19. During the French Wars of Religion, Anne de Montmorency, François de Guise, and Jacques d'Albon de Saint-André, Catholic leaders who had previously been enemies, formed an alliance, disparagingly called the Triumvirate by Protestants.

20. Montmorency led the Catholic troops to victory just north of Paris in 1567, but was mortally wounded during this battle.

21. This term designates moderates who agreed with the politics of compromise supported by Michel de l'Hôpital.

22. Philip II (1527–1598), the only son of the Emperor Charles V and Isabella of Portugal, king of Spain (1555–1598). He remained uncompromisingly Catholic and defended the Catholic faith throughout the world Europe.

Even without fighting on the battlefield, Jeanne knew that she could be active by managing the finances of the Protestant party in the war to come.

Likewise, recent history could lead her to expect a role in the negotiations that would inevitably ensue. Negotiating peace would be completely in keeping with gender roles of the time. During the War of 1562–1563, Condé's first mother-in-law, Madeleine de Mailly, comtesse de Roye, was chosen by the party leaders to negotiate on their behalf with the German Protestant princes. She and her daughter Éléonore, the Princesse de Condé, also participated in the negotiations of the Edict of Amboise, which ended the war in March 1563. Another noblewoman, Jacqueline de Rohan, Marquise de Rothelin, Condé's second mother-in-law, assumed a similar role during the Second War of Religion.[23] When Catherine de' Medici tried to lure Jeanne to court in 1568 by asking her to help mediate between Protestants and Catholics, the queen mother was tempting her with a credible role fashioned to appeal to a woman conscious of her unique rank.[24] Although Jeanne no longer believed that Catherine and Charles IX would entrust her with these responsibilities in 1568, she knew that she would be central to diplomatic decision-making if she chose to join Condé and Coligny.

In Jeanne's case, as a reigning sovereign, her diplomatic role would, in fact, extend far beyond the negotiation of peace. Jeanne already had established diplomatic relations with Elizabeth I of England, a fellow Protestant queen. Although Elizabeth's religious sympathies were tempered by her political needs and her territorial ambitions in France, she remained a vital ally. Condé did not have the official status to negotiate with a foreign queen that Jeanne had, and he had been unsuccessful in securing Elizabeth's aid during the Second War of Religion. Jeanne would know that her requests were more likely to be honored. And indeed, she would acquire important loans and a certain degree of international legitimacy from Elizabeth I in the Third War of Religion.

Religious Promise and Pressure

This overview of the personal, political, economic and military considerations that may have influenced Jeanne in 1568 does not imply that her religious motivations were any less pivotal. It is impossible to separate religious factors from other ones in the context in which Jeanne acted. Jeanne herself had little incentive to try to disentangle motivations that reinforced each other in 1568; her official court historian, Bordenave, cites Jeanne as stating that the attacks against her in 1568 "apparently committed against the Reformed religion, were in fact intended

23. Nancy Lyman Roelker, "The Appeal of Calvinism to French Noblewomen in the Sixteenth Century," *Journal of Interdisciplinary History* 2, no. 4 (1972): 402.
24. See *Ample Declaration*, 199–202.

to abolish the House of Bourbon,"[25] and this sentiment is echoed throughout the *Ample Declaration*.[26]

Jeanne was in regular communication with the leaders of the Protestant city-state of Geneva, requesting spiritual advice and practical support. Théodore de Bèze,[27] who had succeeded John Calvin in 1564, was French, too, and, like Jeanne, noble. He had played a central role in Catherine de' Medici's attempt to reconcile the religious differences between Protestants and Catholics at the 1560 Colloquy of Poissy and had served as a diplomat for the Protestant cause during the First War of Religion. Under his leadership in Geneva, the French situation remained a central concern.[28] Bèze's direct political influence over the French Protestant nobles, however, diminished greatly during the Second War of Religion as Condé took over what he saw as his aristocratic purview. Coligny and Jeanne may have been more open to counsel from this trusted ally in Geneva, but no doubt shared Condé's sense of political entitlement. Bèze did not have the resources to send troops or money to the French Protestants, but Jeanne continued to rely on his encouragement and spiritual guidance. And Bèze, like Calvin before him, maintained pressure on Jeanne to lead French Protestants by public example.

Religion and politics also overlapped in the relationships between Jeanne and those who depended on her in her sovereign lands. Although her traditional clientage network may have been shaken by 1568, as has been seen, bonds with others among her household members, local professionals, and fellow French noblemen had become tighter through the shared cause of defending the Reformed church. Jeanne could count on strengthened loyalty from nobles and non-nobles who already shared common economic and political interests and who were further united by religious beliefs. The number of people who entered Jeanne's employment after her declaration of Protestant beliefs steadily increased until 1568 when she was forced to diminish her household and redirect her finances. The earlier growth suggests the formation of a Protestant community of mutual support centered around Jeanne. Members of her personal household and

25. Nicolas de Bordenave, *Histoire de Béarn et Navarre: 1517 à 1572*, ed. Paul Raymond (Paris: Mme Veuve Jules Renouard, 1873), 154: "fait[s] en aparence contre la religion réformée, estoit en effect pour abolir la maison de Bourbon."

26. See, for example, *Ample Declaration*, 221 or Jeanne's argumentation on pages 225–28.

27. Bèze (1519–1605) was a reformed theologian and French scholar who greatly contributed to the development of humanism and played a key role during the formative years of the Calvinist Reformation in both Geneva and France.

28. Robert M. Kingdon, *Geneva and the Consolidation of the French Protestant Movement, 1564–1572: A Contribution to the History of Congregationalism, Presbyterianism, and Calvinist Resistance Theory* (Madison: University of Wisconsin Press, 1967), 13–14.

clients[29] who would follow her to La Rochelle became resources for the Protestant war effort.

Mutual support and protection were necessary in a climate of constant violence. Frustrated by the edicts and peace negotiations that ignored the aspirations of both Catholics and Protestants outside of the noble class, crowds were taking justice into their own hands. Evangelizing pastors and apocalypse-evoking priests fueled dangerous fears on both sides and could not be controlled politically. A Protestant mob in Nîmes, for example, massacred between twenty and ninety Catholics[30] during the Michelade of September 1567. And Catholics in Paris, fearing a Protestant attack on October 1, 1567, retaliated violently against remaining Protestant residents in what Barbara Diefendorf calls a "rehearsal"[31] for the the the Saint Bartholomew's Day Massacre. Aggravating these passions were food shortages that coincided with iconoclastic violence in the Netherlands in 1566. Developing, too, in 1567 and 1568 were local military confraternities, pious organizations that also sometimes served as Catholic militias targeting Protestants.[32] In the light of such violence, the return of war must have seemed inevitable.

The Protestant churches in France, however, were well poised to respond. Some had been in existence since at least 1555 and they were tightly organized around local consistories and a common set of structural principles agreed upon during the first national synod in Paris in 1559. Historians can only speculate about the numbers of practicing Protestants in France at this moment, but there is compelling evidence that ten percent of French adults may have been part of the Reformed church.[33] The founding documents from 1559, annual meetings of the synods, as well as more frequent ones of regional colloquies, kept these

---

29. Among these faithful friends and *serviteurs* who were engaged in the same religious cause, Jeanne could count many people in her household. Records from 1565 show that Jeanne had 242 people in her paid service, including people of such diverse skills and social rank as doctors, tailors, pastry cooks, stablehands, 13 *femmes de chambre* and 25 *valets de chambre*. Many of these people would maintain links with the Albret household over several generations. Faced with war and with the financial burden that it implied, a large percentage of these *serviteurs* were let in 1568, but those who went with her became resources for the cause. Jeanne's personal treasurer, Jean Bernard, for example, served simultaneously as the treasurer for the Calvinist war effort and others, like Victor Brodeau, served on her council. See J. Russell Major, "Noble Income, Inflation, and the Wars of Religion in France," *American Historical Review* 86, no. 1 (1981): 38–39; Eurich, *The Economics of Power*, 204.

30. Sources agree that the victims were primarily men of the Church although they disagree on the number of people killed. See Allan Tulchin, *That Men Would Praise the Lord: The Triumph of Protestantism in Nîmes, 1530–1570* (Oxford: Oxford University Press, 2010), 170–71.

31. Barbara B. Diefendorf, *Beneath the Cross: Catholics and Huguenots in Sixteenth-Century Paris* (New York: Oxford University Press, 1991), 81.

32. Robert Harding, "The Mobilization of Confraternities against the Reformation in France," *Sixteenth Century Journal* 11, no. 1 (1980): 85–107.

33. Mark Greengrass, *The French Reformation* (Oxford: Basil Blackwell, 1987), 42–43.

numbers united. In order to protect themselves against the mounting violence and to be prepared for an eventual war, military groups were also set up through the churches to facilitate mobilization, and monies were made available to support the Protestant nobles in times of war.

The shifting political and religious landscape of 1568 reveals Jeanne's position in overlapping networks and suggests that her decision to leave for La Rochelle was one consistent with her aspirations as a queen and as a French Protestant. The *Ample Declaration* is then, not only a justificatory memoir, but also an act of war and a refusal to be relegated to a secondary role.

Triumphant March to La Rochelle

On September 6, 1568, Jeanne and her children (fourteen-year-old Henri and nine-year-old Catherine) left the palace at Nérac and traveled to Casteljaloux, accompanied by a relatively small contingent of fifty of her gentlemen. They spent two nights at a house Jeanne maintained there. On September 8, Jeanne slipped away to Tonneins with her children and a small party. Her whereabouts were not secret, however, and she continued to function as queen and as Huguenot leader, receiving the Sieur de La Mothe Fénelon,[34] who stayed at Tonneins September 9 and 10. The group of gentlemen accompanying Jeanne had grown into a small army by the time she left Tonneins, and on September 12, she and her two children triumphantly led the troops into Bergerac. So many Huguenot soldiers joined their ranks that when she left Bergerac for La Rochelle four days later, Jeanne was leading a genuine army. During this part of her voyage she learned that Condé was headed toward her. They met at Archiac on September 23, and Jeanne delivered Henri into Condé's hands, so that the young Prince would take up arms at his uncle's side. Five days later, the Queen and her army, led by Condé and her son, entered La Rochelle in triumph.[35]

Jeanne organized the government of her domains in La Rochelle and created a council with Amiral Coligny and François de la Noue, a Huguenot captain, to reinforce the defenses of the city. She wrote manifestos on behalf of the cause and sent requests for aid to foreign princes. Jeanne was deeply involved in the "general administration of La Rochelle and all aspects of the war that were not strictly military, including finances, fortifications, discipline (except in the army)

---

34. Bertrand de Salignac, Sieur de La Mothe Fénelon, diplomat sent by Charles IX and Catherine de' Medici under the pretense that he would serve as mediator between the Queen of Navarre and her rebellious subjects. In reality, he had been commissioned to bring Jeanne and her son back to the French court. See Bryson, *Queen Jeanne*, 169.

35. Jeanne describes this journey and its culmination at length in her *Ample Declaration*; see 230–38. See also Bryson, *Queen Jeanne*, 189–205 for an analysis of these events.

and, in part, intelligence."[36] Although Jeanne resided in La Rochelle for nearly three years, she did not confine herself to the fortified city, but at times accompanied Coligny to inspect the army and rally the troops.

After having been taken prisoner in the Battle of Jarnac on March 13, 1569, Condé was shot and killed by an officer of the victorious duc d'Anjou (later King Henri III of France).[37] When Jeanne learned of Condé's assassination, she hurriedly traveled to the soldiers' camp to bolster the spirit of the disheartened troops, taking with her two princes of the blood, Condé's son as well as her own, both named Henri. Jeanne was no longer a pacifist queen tending only to her own territories, but was now a sort of regent for the Protestant Party in France.

The Last Years

Jeanne's efforts to rally the Protestant troops and to keep them fighting during the Third War of Religion despite their many military setbacks helped bring Catherine and Charles IX to the negotiating table. She and Coligny were rewarded for their firm negotiating by the Peace of Saint-Germain (1570), a treaty that offered French Protestants more legal rights than any of the previous treaties, added the right to worship in certain, specified towns and kept under Protestant control the fortified towns of La Rochelle, Cognac, Montauban and La Charité-sur-Loire. Although the conditions were favorable, the application of this peace met with great resistance and Jeanne was ultimately disappointed by its impact.

Jeanne devoted the remainder of her life to the advancement of her religion and her son. She participated in negotiations over Henri's marriage to Marguerite de Valois, daughter of Henri II of France and Catherine de' Medici. Although Jeanne wanted Marguerite to convert to Protestantism, Marguerite refused. Increasingly frail, and probably suffering from tuberculosis, Jeanne died in Paris on June 9, 1572, at which point Henri inherited her throne. Jeanne did not live to see her son's marriage to Marguerite on August 18, 1572 nor his ascension to the French throne as King Henri IV in 1589. But her premature death spared her witnessing the horror of the Saint Bartholomew's Day Massacre on August 23, 1572, and what would surely have been the great disappointment of her life, her son's conversion to Catholicism twenty-one years later.

Despite her exceptional political and religious authority and her central role in the Third War of Religion, Jeanne d'Albret's legacy has been largely overshadowed by that of others, notably the literary reputation of her mother, Marguerite de Navarre, and the prominent political position of her son, Henri IV, first Bourbon king of France. This was not true during her lifetime, when Jeanne's skill at

---

36. Roelker, *Queen of Navarre*, 312.

37. Son of Henri II and Catherine de' Medici, born in 1551 as Alexandre Edouard, became King Henri III of France in 1574. His younger brother, François, assumed the title of Duc d'Anjou in 1576.

negotiating and her personal integrity earned praise from her allies and respect from her adversaries. Her clients and fellow Protestants followed her as a valued leader without questioning the limitations of her sex. The author Georgette de Montenay, for example, pays tribute to Jeanne's exemplary life and to its relevance to the Reformed community in her dedication to Jeanne of the *Emblemes ou devises chrestiennes* (1571):

> Que l'Immortel de vous faisant son temple
> Vous façonna pour estre à tous exemple,[38]

Clearly the impact of Jeanne as model extends far beyond this community and the specific conflict of the Wars of Religion. It is hoped that this brief introduction and the translation of the *Ample Declaration* will make evident the continued relevance of Jeanne's significant contributions. She possessed skills that have a particular resonance for the twenty-first-century reader: the ability to balance the responsibilities and roles of political leader, wife, mother, religious dissident and author, as well as the judgment and confidence to champion publicly her cause while protecting the interests of her children.

Other Genre, Other Voice

Other women of her era also needed to balance different roles, but Jeanne d'Albret's privileged rank added a unique complexity to her situation. There were few life models for an early modern woman who assumed so many roles over the course of her life and took on such wide-ranging responsibilities. And there were certainly no truly applicable literary models for such a woman writer. Her female contemporaries wrote poetry and letters. Some elite women wrote memoirs, writings often presented as private and intended only for the author's family. Jeanne's own mother, Marguerite de Navarre, had written religious drama and novellas, but she was the sister of a powerful king who protected her from censure.

Before writing the *Ample Declaration*, Jeanne had few compositions to her name: a poetic exchange with the poet Joachim Du Bellay, a quatrain written to the printer Robert Estienne, some epistolary verses addressed to her mother, and an extensive correspondence with her husband and other key figures of the time. Jeanne, however, possessed a solid literary culture, a strong sense of the language, and a mastery of rhetoric exceptional for a woman of this time. She had specific and indeed critical goals in writing her *Ample Declaration*: to explain, to convince, to defend her decisions, and to inspire her readers to take action. The readers that she anticipated for her text were diverse, first among them the royal family, to

---

38. "God the immortal, in making you his temple, fashioned you as an example for all." Georgette de Montenay, *Emblemes ou devises chrestiennes* (Lyon: Jean Marcovelle, 1571), a2ᵛ; editors' translation).

whom she addressed the letters she seeks to explicate in her *Declaration*. But she wrote also for all of her contemporaries, and in fact for posterity, denouncing her Catholic adversaries and defending her Protestant allies.

Jeanne was keenly sensitive to her historical legacy, and she was faced with strategic decisions as she took up her plume. Which voice would she adopt? That of a queen? of a mother?[39] of a Reformer? What sort of rhetorical strategy would she employ? Which genre or genres would best serve her purpose? One of the most striking features of the *Ample Declaration* is its mosaic of genres; indeed, this text stands at the crossroads of several genres, combining aspects of the epistolary form and the novella, and most significantly, the polemical pamphlet and the memoir.

The Ample Declaration *and the Epistolary Form*

Much has been written about the importance of letter writing for early modern women. Jeanne herself wrote many letters in the course of her life. In 1568, her epistolary activity appears to have been particularly intense. Some of these letters were initially published in La Rochelle to defend Jeanne's decision to find refuge in this Protestant stronghold. In 1569, they were reprinted together with the *Ample Declaration*, which elaborates upon them. It is useful here to compare and contrast the *Ample Declaration* with the letters it was meant to accompany and to analyze the enactment of letter writing omnipresent in this text.

In 1570, when the *Ample Declaration* was published for the third time, it was included in a volume entitled *Histoire de nostre temps*, which contains letters, *remonstrances*, *discours*, and memoir-type documents. Apparently, for sixteenth-century readers, the common political aim of these genres was more significant than the differences that might exist between them. From the outset, the *Ample Declaration* is presented as a means to go beyond genre boundaries. Jeanne claims that she set out to write her *Declaration* because she felt the need to explain certain things more fully than she had previously done in her letters: "I *only briefly mentioned* matters that I wish to make everyone understand more fully. Therefore I took quill in hand to *elaborate upon the principal subject* in these letters, that is to say, the circumstances that forced me to abandon my sovereign lands. … my intention is *to explain in more detail* those motivations that I only outlined in my letters" (173, emphasis ours).

Such detail was required, it seems, not only because of the constraining format of the letter (the length of a letter was kept to a minimum, usually no more

---

39. Recent studies have addressed the question of Jeanne as mother figure. See Margaret L. King, *How Mothers Shaped Successful Sons and Created World History: The School of Infancy* (Lewiston NY: The Edwin Mellen Press, 2014), 195–96 and 446, and Marian Rothstein's forthcoming book on the androgyne.

than one side of a sheet of paper[40]), but also because of the inherent limitations of epistolary exchanges, as Jeanne explains more fully in her *Declaration*. For many reasons, some messages could not be explicitly written or even written at all, and needed to be delivered orally by the bearers of abbreviated letters "intended to be merely introductions for the bearers, who were charged with speaking the senders' actual messages."[41] In a similar manner, the *Declaration* was intended to provide further information (this was the principal meaning of the word *declaration* at that time) for those to whom Jeanne had previously written letters (her relatives, the Royal family, her religious and political allies), filling in the blanks and reveal-ing what could not be said explicitly in her letters. Whereas the letters were meant to be read together with the *Ample Declaration* since they complement each other, the *Ample Declaration* can be read separately, even though it frequently refers to these letters: "As I said in my letter to the queen of England" (227); "as I said in my letter to the queen" (233).

The *Ample Declaration* shares many of the features of the epistolary genre. The most striking feature common to both genres is traces of orality,[42] which attest to the survival of oral culture in sixteenth-century France. Many of the stylistic features found in the letters are present in the *Declaration*. Among these, one observes the predilection for redundancy in the form of repetitive construction, emphasis for the sake of comprehension as shown by the repeated use of pairs of words, and "the grafting of subsequent, often unrelated, thoughts to previous ones," which is, according to Kristen B. Neuschel,[43] typical of oral expression. Di-rect address is also a common trait of both the letters and the *Declaration*. Even though no one is actually designated as the recipient of the *Declaration*, one has the impression in reading this text that Jeanne is addressing the queen mother in particular. On one occasion she even says, "Hoping that one day she [the Queen] will read this" (180).

A characteristic of early modern women's correspondence, accord-ing to Jane Couchman,[44] is the impossibility of separating private from public. This feature seems more striking in the *Declaration* than in the letters. Jeanne

---

40. James Daybell, "'I wold wyshe my doings myght be … secret': Privacy and the Social Practices of Reading Women's Letters in Sixteenth-Century England," in *Women's Letters Across Europe, 1400–1700. Form and Persuasion*, ed. Jane Couchman and Ann Crabb (Aldershot: Ashgate, UK, 2005), 158.

41. Kristen B. Neuschel, *Word of Honor: Interpreting Noble Culture in Sixteenth-Century France* (Ithaca: Cornell University Press, 1989), 114.

42. See Daybell, "I wold whyshe," 160: "The emphasis on rhetoric in Renaissance humanist letter-writing manuals strongly suggests that letters were often drafted with the intention that they be read aloud."

43. Neuschel, *Word of Honor*, 104.

44. Jane Couchman, "What is 'Personal' about Sixteenth-Century French Women's Personal Writings?" *Atlantis* 19, no. 1 (1993): 16–22.

occasionally speaks of private matters such as her health and her feelings for her husband and her children, but she never expands on her private life and instead devotes the larger part of her *Declaration* to political events (uprisings, edicts, machinations of the Guise brothers, taking up of arms by the Protestants and so forth). Furthermore, the private matters that she mentions always have a direct impact on the public events recounted. Her illness, for example, prevents her from accompanying Catherine de' Medici to her meeting with the Spanish ambassador in Bayonne. The construction of her self-image as a devoted mother makes even more horrible the machinations of her enemies as they tried to wrench her son away from her.

Another element that gives the *Declaration* a private dimension is the references to people or events only known to some (the implied correspondents) and the secrecy surrounding certain facts. And yet, these silences, dictated by the need to protect the identity of some individuals, could also mean that Jeanne was trying to make her *Declaration* suitable for wider dissemination, foreseeing that it would someday become *public*: "It may be superfluous to speak about my own affairs, nonetheless, *to make known to everyone* the long-standing malice of the Cardinal de Lorraine and his brother the Sieur de Guise, I will say …" (186); "I want *people* to examine impartially …" (229, emphasis ours).

This idea of an expanded readership is corroborated by the motivations alleged by Jeanne in writing her correspondence and her *Declaration*. In both, she claims that her intention is to show the truth in broad daylight, to give a fuller explanation in order to justify her actions and rehabilitate her image. Self-justification, which seems to be here the predominant motivation, is also characteristic of the other genres (the pamphlet and the memoir) that Jeanne so masterfully appropriates in her *Declaration*.

The *Ample Declaration* not only shares many traits with the letters published along with it; in addition, it provides valuable insight into both the composition of these letters and the evolving epistolary genre as a whole. The *Ample Declaration* includes information regarding the date when Jeanne wrote the letters, the circumstances in which she wrote, and her real intentions in doing so: "I kept La Mothe at Bergerac Monday, Tuesday, and Wednesday, while I wrote letters, which he was to deliver to Monsieur le Prince my brother-in-law, to their majesties, to Monsieur brother of the King, and to Monsieur le Cardinal, my brother-in-law. Anyone can read these letters in print, but because they seemed to me *too brief*, I decided to declare clearly my purpose by writing *this expanded treatise*" (236, emphasis ours). It also tells us a great deal about Jeanne's epistolary exchanges during this tumultuous time with her brother-in-law, the Prince de Condé, in order to maintain her network of *sodalitas* and with the king and queen mother, including the content of the letters she sent to their majesties and the answers she received.

By mentioning letters she wrote to the king and queen, Jeanne shows that she did everything she could to avoid civil and religious conflicts: "I wrote to them about the fear I had that all of this would make us fall back into misfortune. I remonstrated with them in complete humility, as their most humble servant, driven by duty to protect the peace and best interests of this kingdom" (203). Elsewhere, references to her epistolary exchange with the queen through the intermediary of La Mothe are meant to show how her enemies, with the queen's support, tried to lure her back to court under the pretense that she could play a key role in the conservation of peace (see 204–6). Finally, the *Ample Declaration* is a revealing window into the epistolary practices of the time. Much is said about specific letters, when, how, why they were written, delivered, received, read, etc. As letters could have a crucial impact on the political scene, precautions were taken at the time in writing, delivering, or keeping letters in one's possession.

Several passages in the *Declaration* shed light on the circumstances in which letters were written. We learn for instance that letters were frequently written while others were around. This lack of privacy obviously played a major role in what was said and how it was said. Sometimes the presence of others created such pressure that the writer felt compelled to say the opposite of what he or she meant: "I sent Brandon back to the Queen, and when he returned he brought me some letters in which she commanded me to ask Monsieur le Prince my brother-in-law to lay down his arms. However, the opinion of the messenger was that d'Escars, having entered her chamber in order to make her write that letter, had not left her side while she was writing. This was the reason why she was forced to write the opposite of the opinion she had expressed to the gentleman" (184).

Form and style were affected by the purpose of the letter and its recipient. Jeanne mentions over and over again the humble way in which she addresses the king and queen in her letters, which was her way of showing what a respectful, obedient, and loyal subject she was: "I remember that in my letter to the queen I used the same or similar words, beseeching her humbly to recognize those who had always been devoted to the service of the crown" (197). Besides the *civilités obligées*, we learn about the importance of the language used in letters, for words can easily be interpreted in the wrong way. On one occasion, Jeanne calls our attention to the words used by the queen about the Protestants in her letter to the king of Spain. For Jeanne, these words showed that Protestants were viewed as rebels, but the queen gave Jeanne another explanation, insisting on a diplomatic and historical context for her words.

One of the principal aims of letters was to share information: "I also knew about the strange rebellion in Béarn and later in Navarre of a few of my subjects backed by France (apparent in the letters that their majesties wrote to them)" (196); "The Sieur de La Mothe … brought me letters from them [their majesties], informing me that my brother-in-law had been taken prisoner, and that Monsieur l'Amiral was with him" (232). Another important aim was to spread ideas that could lead to action, bring about some action or reaction on the part of the correspondent and thus have an impact on the world. But on several occasions, Jeanne regretfully admits that her letters to the king and queen did not have the effect anticipated: "I could speak of my legitimate complaints, which motivated me to write many letters without ever obtaining satisfaction" (193); "[Voupillieres] brought me a very strange response, far removed from the hope that La Mothe had tried to give me" (206).

In her *Declaration*, Jeanne mentions another aspect of the performative potential of letters. In time of conflict, letters could indeed be utilized as a stratagem to cause suspicion and confuse adversaries: "Through him [the Sieur de Bouchavannes] she [the queen] instructed me with much firmness ... to send one of my men secretly to the Prince de Condé, my brother-in-law, and Monsieur l'Amiral to warn them not to believe anything signed by the king, nor sealed with his seal, for from that time on he would be doing everything under duress" (182). The queen mother seems particularly mindful of the risk associated with the epistolary medium. On more than one occasion, Jeanne reports the queen's strict instructions to her as to the manner by which their letters to each other should be dispatched: "they [The king and queen] commanded me to identify one of my men through whom we could communicate, either with letters of credence, or should I trust him, without a letter, about how best to serve them" (183). Jeanne goes to great lengths to tell her readers how letter-bearers were designated, what their role was, and how well they accomplished the mission with which they had been entrusted.

For reasons of security and also because of a continued reliance on the spoken word,[45] letters containing sensitive information were often accompanied by letters of credence guaranteeing the reliability of the letter-bearer who could confirm the content of the letter. The role of the letter-bearer went beyond that of delivering the letter to the addressee. When sensitive material had consciously been left out, he was charged to convey orally what had been omitted, which he did not always do: "in my opinion [La Mothe] did not tell me everything that he was supposed to" (232). He could also report how he found the recipient. Jeanne learns this way how Condé was forced to leave his home in order to avoid being captured: "my messenger recounted to me the way they departed and their journey across the fields ..." (212). Letters delivered were frequently read aloud by someone other than the recipient and sometimes in the company of other people, like the letter the queen had the Sieur de l'Aubespine read to her in the presence of Madame de Savoie (188).

Being in possession of letters could cause just as much apprehension as writing or dispatching letters. Leaving a material trace, a letter could be used as a tangible proof to harm a reputation or impair political interests. The letter from

---

45. Neuschel, *Word of Honor*, 103–31.

Cardinal de Crequy's agent was sufficient proof to incriminate the Cardinal de Lorraine: "The cardinal's plot has in fact since been unmasked by the letter from Cardinal de Crequy's agent" (31). But letters could also be used as proof of one's good intentions. In trying to explain why she disobeyed the king and queen when they asked her to deliver a message from them to her brother-in-law as she passed through Orléans, Jeanne claims that her husband forbade her to do so and that she has a letter from him to prove it: "The late king my husband expressly forbade this (I still have the letter in this regard)" (183). When Jeanne had reason to be suspicious of one of her husband's secretaries, a certain Boulogne, she had him arrested and she confiscated "his packet of letters" (186). Letters, indeed, could end up in the wrong hands as did that letter found amid debris by Jeanne's little dog. This discovery nearly caused a diplomatic incident. Jeanne initially hesitated to read the letter, aware of the political implications and personal risks inherent in the mere possession of such a letter (188–90).

In sum, the *Declaration* provides ample information about Jeanne's epistolary activity during the crucial year of 1568, important clues to the intentions behind her writing, and an interesting perspective on the epistolary form and sixteenth-century epistolary practices.

The Novellas in the Ample Declaration

"I will tell you," Jeanne assures her readers with a simple phrase that evokes an oral storytelling scenario. Jeanne's mother, Marguerite de Navarre, punctuates her famous collection of novellas, the *Heptaméron*,[46] with the same phrase. What other connections exist between a text Jeanne obsessively claims is true on the one hand and, on the other, the tradition of oral storytelling and the written fiction that closely mimics it? According to Neuschel, sixteenth-century nobles organized knowledge in narrative form, what she calls, "the dramaturgic expression of and creation of meaning."[47] Jeanne goes beyond this early modern cognitive habit to deliberately exploit literary traditions of storytelling in certain parts of the *Ample Declaration*. She was certainly familiar with the *Heptaméron* (published posthumously in 1558) and appears to have played a central role in the early editions of her mother's novellas.[48]

The short story in prose was a popular genre in France even before the publishing of the *Heptaméron*. Philippe de Vigneulles wrote the earliest known French collection entitled the *Cent Nouvelles Nouvelles* in 1462. His stories draw

46. Marguerite de Navarre, *The Heptameron*, trans. Paul A. Chilton (London: Penguin Books, 1984).
47. Neuschel, *Word of Honor*, 122.
48. See, for example, Nicole Cazauran, "Boaistuau et Gruget éditeurs de *l'Heptaméron*: À chacun sa part," *Travaux de littérature* 14 (2001): 149–69, and Michel Simonin, "Notes sur Pierre Boaistuau," *Bibliothèque d'Humanisme et Renaissance* 38 (1976): 323–33.

from the oral tradition and from the fabliaux, placing these conventional stories in the regional context of Burgundy. Bonaventure Des Périers's *Nouvelles Récréations et Joyeux Devis* added classical *facetiae* as well as Italian tales to the mix of sources, but also situated his stories firmly in the regions of France. Both of these writers favored comic tales, although Des Périers hints at more serious underlying linguistic and religious themes. The *Heptaméron* serves as a bridge to later collections that turn more completely to Boccaccio's *Decameron* (ca 1353) for inspiration and include elaborate frame stories. By 1559 the fictional story genre in France had embraced tragic themes and longer stories as can be found in the translations of Bandello by Pierre Boaistuau and François de Belleforest.

The popularity of this genre in France throughout the sixteenth century is undeniable. Much more difficult to establish, however, is a clear definition or even an undisputed term for these stories. Short prose fiction was published under multiple names—histories, novellas, *devis, contes/compte*—and they recycle elements from an even more diverse set of fictional and non-fictional genres. This flexible literary form offered Jeanne several advantages. Its popularity and its reliance on informal discourse rendered it accessible to a wide readership. Dramatizing events and structuring them into narrative modules provided Jeanne with a striking and mnemonic evocation of specific historical moments. Finally, these stories were well adapted to the rhetorical devices that Jeanne employs throughout the *Ample Declaration*, like her use of the *exemplum* to persuade, justify, and blame.

The entire *Ample Declaration* tells a story, of course: that of the exemplary life of Jeanne d'Albret. But Jeanne embeds shorter tales (one to four pages) within her text that also serve as examples. That is to say, they are illustrations of an argument, they provide proof for this argument, and they suggest paragons of behavior (either to emulate or to avoid).[49] An example, by definition, must be separated from a larger whole. The embedded stories within the *Ample Declaration* are separated from the rest of the text through the use of labels or through interruptions in the narrative theme or chronology.

A second way Jeanne distinguished these forms is by using them to include voices other than her own through either direct or indirect discourse. Her reliance on dialogue in these passages evokes an oral tradition of storytelling and a theme of communication and its challenges typical of the novella.

A third and final trait that distinguishes stories in the *Ample Declaration* is the presence of a minimal but distinct plot and a specific setting. These elements further separate the story from the surrounding prose and reproduce the structure of the novella. Sometimes one or even two of these elements may be present in the *Ample Declaration*, but only four passages contain all three aspects. In Story

---

49. John Lyons, *Exemplum: The Rhetoric of Example in Early Modern France and Italy* (Princeton: Princeton University Press, 1989), 6–20.

1, entitled for clarification "The Attempted Murder" (175–79), Jeanne tells of a plot hatched by the Guises to have King François II assassinate Antoine de Bourbon. She describes the confrontation and Antoine's successful overcoming of this threat. In Story 2, "The Purloined Letter" (187–91), Jeanne recounts the discovery of a letter written by the queen mother to the king of Spain and the duplicitous behaviors revealed by the surprising apparition of this letter. Story 3, "The Silenced Assassin" (192–93), describes the assassination of a man named Savigny and the mysterious disappearance of his imprisoned murderer. Finally, Story 4, "The Inspired Son," showcases in a few lines (at 234–35) the wit of Jeanne's son, Henri.

Jeanne brings attention to a break in her discourse through disrupted chronology or argumentation and through vocabulary that signals a narrative shift. She further delineates two of the stories to which she assigns particular labels. The "Attempted Murder" is termed by Jeanne a "tragicomedy" and "The Inspired Son," a *comte* ("tale"). Even though these words could theoretically refer to several different kinds of narrative forms,[50] here they are clearly reminiscent of literary genres. The term "tragédie" might at first seem to point to different kind of fiction. But, starting in 1559 under the collective title, *Histoires Tragiques*, several extremely popular volumes of French translations of Bandello's tales had revitalized the short story genre in France. These stories in turn inspired several tragic plays.

Given fluid literary terminology and categorization during Jeanne's lifetime, her use of *tragicomedie* in no way excludes consideration of the novella. Nor, by using the terms *comtes* and *tragicomedie*, is Jeanne opposing fiction to history, for she believes that these literary forms, too, can express "the naked truth" (175). If Jeanne stops short of claiming the role of historian, it is the length of the chronicles that she rejects as she makes clear after recounting the story about her son, "not to boast about him, nor to act as his historiographer" (235), but simply to provide an example of Henri's independence.

In order for Jeanne's stories to serve as credible examples, however, they need to appear true and verifiable. Inserting the words of others into these stories, paradoxical as it might seem, aids Jeanne in persuading her readers of her reliability as a narrator. First the use of direct discourse creates a sense of immediacy that lends a greater verisimilitude to these stories. Secondly, the use of direct or indirect discourse can concisely and compellingly depict the personalities of Jeanne's family members as well as her enemies. Readers can then draw the conclusions that Jeanne wants them to draw before or even without her overt intervention. In the first story, for example, dialogue allows her to illustrate her husband's

---

50. A *comte* (or *conte* or *compte*) at the time referred simply to a narration, a recounted story that could be either true, or deceitful; serious or meant to entertain. And though the term *comédie* would very quickly be defined exclusively in terms of fiction and theatre, in the sixteenth century, it could still refer to a speech or sermon. See, for example, *DMF : Dictionnaire du Moyen Français, version 2012 (DMF 2012). ATILF—CNRS & Université de Lorraine.* Site internet : http://www.atilf.fr/dmf.

courage and magnanimity in a few words as well as to exploit the forcefulness of his language. She also manages to suggest the infamy of the Guises by attributing a treasonous insult to them. She cites them as disparaging the king for having failed to kill Antoine, "Here is the most cowardly heart there ever was" (178), before reinterpreting cowardice as the act of killing one's own relatives. That this use of direct discourse is a rhetorical device and not a simple transcription is obvious from the fact that Jeanne herself was not present at this scene. She also attributes the condemnation of the king to both the Cardinal de Lorraine and his brother the duc de Guise (suggesting either that they spoke simultaneously or that there was no need to distinguish between her two enemies). Although this use of the direct discourse does not necessarily conform to a strict reality, it lends credence to Jeanne's characterization of those who utter it.

In addition to their structural and discursive differences, all four stories contain elements of a basic plot (that of a confrontation) and specific temporal and spatial settings. Jeanne constructs her stories of confrontation around traditional novella storylines, thus making these events readily intelligible to readers. One theme common to both the Italian and the early French novellas is that of clever repartee. These stories do not constitute a sequence of actions, but instead dramatize a clever dialogue. The story Jeanne tells of Henri fits into this pattern. When the young Henri assures La Mothe that, with a simple pail of water, he could put an end to the fiery religious wars in France "by making the Cardinal de Lorraine drink until he bursts," (235) he wins a recognizable battle of wits. Jeanne can thus use this familiar fictional scenario to ensure that readers side with her young, yet articulate son, bravely confronting with his wit alone the authority figures represented by La Mothe and the cardinal.

Another typical novella plot is that of the unwitting revelation of a character's deceit. When she recounts the story of the pet dog that accidentally reveals the Guises' illicit possession of a letter written by the queen mother, Jeanne can exploit a literary genre that primes readers to sympathize once more with the victorious underdog. In this case, the underdog is quite literally a dog, an animal that also provides Jeanne with a symbol for loyalty[51] and thus further emphasizes Jeanne's own loyalty contrasted with the duplicity of the Guises and of the queen mother.

"The Attempted Murder" is a more complex story and the longest of the four. Rather than drawing from the comic tradition or stories that focus on verbal exchanges, Jeanne sets up a potentially tragic scenario with a hero (Antoine) who consciously puts himself in the hands of his enemies out of bravery and feudal loyalty. Like the model tragic story, this tale is openly didactic (reinforcing

51. For the multivalency of the symbol of the dog (associated with both loyalty and heresy) in medieval texts see Ben Ramm, "Barking up the Wrong Tree? The Significance of the *Chienet* in Old French Romance," *Parergon* 22, no. 1 (2005): 47–69.

a conservative chivalric code) and transforms violence into spectacle. Antoine evokes his soon-to-be bloodied shirt, a shirt he wishes Jeanne to display to Christian princes so they will avenge his death. Jeanne, as narrator, conjures up more bloody imagery when she laments the wickedness of those who would sully the king's hand with the blood of a fellow French prince. The anticipated act of violence however fails to take place.

Instead, the act of murder in the *Ample Declaration* is displaced to another story, "The Silenced Assassin," where two assassinations take place. Whereas the other three embedded stories celebrate triumphant moments for Jeanne, "The Silenced Assassin" is closer to Jeanne's general focus on disaster, both past and imminent. It, too, is the only story that does not feature someone from Jeanne's immediate family in a leading role. Savigny, the first victim, is said to be considered Antoine's bastard son, but Jeanne does not openly acknowledge him as such. A hapless victim, his role is moreover secondary to that of the "foreign" villains: the Guises,[52] the Spanish assassin, and a mysterious Italian who represents the person ultimately responsible for all the bloodshed.

Thus Jeanne's stories reflect both the early, comic tradition that is placed in a specifically French setting and the *histoire tragique* that more openly avows its debt to Italian literary models. A reading of the two tragic stories together suggests an underlying political message. Although the Italian queen mother, Catherine de' Medici, tries to avoid the first assassination by acting against the Guises and warning Antoine, she becomes the instrument of the Guises and the enabler of the assassinations in the story that occurs a few years later. In "The Attempted Murder," the hero, Antoine, is not guilty of a transgression—he tries to heed the warnings he is given, but eventually obeys the orders of his king. As he has not transgressed, he cannot be punished. He and François II, both kings and both French, are protected by divine intervention. Jeanne's rewriting of the typical Italian novella brings it closer to the alternate model for novellas: one where tragedy is replaced by verbal dueling ("the confrontation played out in words," 178) and where specifically French virtues are celebrated (Béarnais wit and the frankness of the French nobility as incarnated by Jeanne). In the case of the "Silenced Assassin," however, the foreign cabal succeeds in enacting the expected Italian plot. If, as Timothy Hampton argues, novellas establish a type of national narrative using historical events,[53] Jeanne's stories transform events so as to reinforce Protestant propaganda and frame the Guises and Catherine as increasingly nefarious, non-native influences.

The tragic novellas also provide Jeanne with a moralistic, prescriptive presentation for her stories. Whereas authors of earlier story collections problematized

52. The opponents of the Guises insisted on the non-French origins of the House of Lorraine in order to discredit them.

53. Timothy Hampton, "Examples, Stories, and Subjects in *Don Quixote* and the *Heptameron,*" *Journal of the History of Ideas* 59, no. 4 (1998): 597–611.

the exemplarity of their tales, she restrains the polysemy of her narratives so that they clearly convey specific religious and political ideas. Thus she guides her readers in the deciphering of her examples, giving them no interpretative leeway and eliminating any competing conclusions to her stories. She explains the intent of each story before she tells it and draws the conclusion for the readers afterwards. "The Attempted Murder," for example, is meant to provide evidence of the Guises' wickedness: "among an infinite number of examples of suffering and humiliation and dishonor that [the Guises] inflicted on him, I will recount one here" (175).

If this example is meant as an illustration of an argument, "The Inspired Son," serves as an example that can prove her son's devotion and persuade readers of the same; the story lets "everyone know that he did not come to this cause as a child led by his mother, but that his own innate will was joined with mine because he recognized the excellence of that cause" (235). Both stories also provide models of behavior either to emulate (Antoine for his bravery, Henri for his wit) or to avoid (the Guises for their treachery). "The Silenced Assassin," too, describes evil actors whose actions should not be imitated and once again illustrates the malicious scheming of the Guises: "And that is how these evil souls want to shake up heaven and earth, and by their malice overthrow piety and justice, and poison the mind of our young, naturally good king with their venomous temperament" (193).

In "The Purloined Letter," the meaning of the written word is temporarily thrown into doubt. Catherine disavows her earlier portrayal of Protestants and she and her courtiers are unsure even how to interpret the letter as a sign without knowing who is responsible for putting it back into circulation: "some said that some Huguenots had had it stolen, others said that it was Catholics who had done so, and still others said that some foreign ambassador had procured it in order to incite us against one another. However, none of them was on the mark" (189). For Jeanne, however, there is a "mark," a correct explanation for the letter's apparition and a single meaning for its content. Jeanne has already stated the meaning that she targets at the beginning of the story; in a way that leaves no opportunity for debate, she declares, "[this story] will lead any Christian of good judgment to admire the Providence of Almighty God. He surprises the clever in their cleverness, and the wise of the world in their wisdom by using means both surprising and feeble to vanquish the strong" (187). In their guided and certain exemplarity, Jeanne's stories complement the rest of the *Ample Declaration* where she likewise pressures her readers to accept judgments she presents as facts that "everyone knows" (195) already.

Jeanne is not alone among authors in the 1560s to adapt novellas to frame texts of a decidedly religious and or political nature.[54] Both Protestant ministers

---

54. See Henri Estienne, *L'introduction au traité de la conformité des merveilles anciennes avec les modernes ou, Traité preparatif à l'Apologie pour Hérodote*, ed. Bénédicte Boudou (Geneva : Droz, 2007).

and Catholic preachers likewise continued to insert stories with a didactic, propagandistic intent into sermons and books as exempla. There is no need to see
Jeanne as reverting to a medieval notion of exemplarity, for as the scholars who
debated the question in the 1998 *Journal of the History of Ideas* concur, "The Renaissance crisis of exemplarity ends in a complicated copresence of exemplarity
and its problematization."[55]

In fact, Jeanne's adaptation of the novella reveals a keen understanding both
of fourteenth- and fifteenth-century prose fiction as well as the evolution of the
genre in the 1560s. Jeanne skillfully exploits the rhetorical power of the novella
and the nationalistic implications of certain plots. Like her mother, she uses prose
narrative to further her own aims in a unique and compelling way. Although she
ultimately rejects both the rhetorical flourishes of the tragic novella and the levity
of the comic tale, familiar elements from these literary forms help her persuade
her readers of the righteousness of her political and religious views.

The Ample Declaration *and Protestant Polemic*

If the storytelling aspect of the *Ample Declaration* helped Jeanne reach a broader
readership, the aim of her text was not to delight, but to instruct and to persuade.
In order to convince wavering Protestants and moderate Catholics throughout
France that the military response of the Protestant Party was just and patriotic, to
counter the accusations of Catholic preachers and the tarnishing of her reputation, Jeanne needed to circulate widely her political and religious perspectives.
She was well aware of the war of printed words waged effectively on both sides
of the religious conflict. Like much of the religious propaganda printed during
the Wars of Religion,[56] the *Ample Declaration* constitutes a direct response to a
specific adversarial text, in Jeanne's case Antoine Fleury's tract demonizing the
Amiral Coligny.[57] At regular intervals, Jeanne refers her readers to other recent
printed works for further information about Condé's trials, the royal family's actions, or the purportedly presumptuous and treasonous goals of Guise supporters.
The decision to write the *Ample Declaration* is itself an acknowledgment of the
importance of printed propaganda in the war effort. Évelyne Berriot-Salvadore
praises the understanding of her time that Jeanne displays by using writing as

---

55. These critics concur that despite a growing recognition during the Renaissance of the polysemy of
signs and of texts, the end of the sixteenth century does not mark a complete departure from the use
of literary exempla. See Karlheinz Stierle, "Three Moments in the Crisis of Exemplarity: Boccaccio-
Petrarch, Montaigne, and Cervantes," *Journal of the History of Ideas* 59, no. 4 (1998): 583–95.

56. Geneviève Guilleminot, "La polémique en 1561: Les règles du jeu," in *Le pamphlet en France au
XVIe siècle* (Paris: Ecole normale supérieure de jeunes filles, 1983), 49.

57. Antoine Fleury, *Response à un certain escrit publié par l'Admiral et ses adherans pretendans couvrir
et excuser la rupture qu'ils ont faicte de l'edict de pacification* (Paris, chez Claude Fremy, 1568).

a political weapon.[58] The letters traditionally used to maintain diplomatic relations and to plead one's political case were no longer sufficient. Within the *Ample Declaration*, Jeanne complains that her letters have received no response and expresses doubts that some of them have reached their intended destination or been publicly shared as she intended.

The style, tone, and imagery of the *Ample Declaration* contribute to the impression that this text, like the Protestant polemic of the era, was designed to sway the emerging public opinion and vilify Catholics while rehabilitating the image of Protestants. In *Hatred in Print*, Luc Racaut argues that the failed Conspiracy of Amboise in 1562 greatly damaged the credibility of the Protestants.[59] Till then, Protestants had portrayed themselves as innocent martyrs, associating their destiny with that of the early Church. But after Amboise, Protestants, now termed political criminals by Catholics, were forced to respond to accusations of rebellion and lèse-majesté.

In the *Ample Declaration*, the polemical character of the rhetoric is clear. Everything is presented in terms of black and white, of extremes, of the sharpest of contrasts, a trait typical of propaganda literature as Racaut[60] and Peter Matheson[61] remind us. Protestants were accused by Catholics of being "traitors, rebels, and subversives (188, 214), Jeanne portrays them instead as "trustworthy servants of their God and monarch" (193, 209, 229). While Protestants are shown to serve their king and country as loyal subjects should do, their enemies are depicted as "these rebels who have broken his edicts and defied his commands" (213). On another occasion, Jeanne declares that she could not possibly sojourn at court while the Cardinal de Lorraine is there, for her fidelity and his infidelity are totally incompatible (202). The repetition over and over again of these sharp polarities, as if Jeanne is trying to engrave them in collective memory, continually reinforces the message that a radical choice has to be made between good and bad, falsehoods and the True Religion, Satan and God (215). What transpires through such dualism is the similarity of the two sides' self-images. This is the most striking feature of the French politico-religious debate of the late sixteenth century. In her seminal study of the polemical battle between Protestants and Catholics, Sara K. Barker notes:

---

58. Évelyne Berriot-Salvadore, *Les femmes dans la société française de la Renaissance* (Geneva: Droz, 1990), 410.

59. Luc Racaut, *Hatred in Print: Catholic Propaganda and Protestant Identity during the French Wars of Religion* (Aldershot, UK: Ashgate, 2002), 67–68. It is at that time that the Protestants of France began to be called Huguenots (67).

60. Racaut, *Hatred in Print*, 44.

61. Peter Matheson, *The Rhetoric of Reformation* (Edinburgh: T&T Clark, 1998), 145.

Both Catholics and Protestants held the same values dear: those of order, loyalty to one's country and monarch, and the fundamental greatness of the French nation. Both despised disorder and disloyalty. Where their consensus broke down was over the minutiae of theology, minutiae which proved to be so important that each side's adherence to the same values made them implacable enemies with little hope of reconciliation.[62]

Jeanne uses the motif of the world turned upside down, widespread in sixteenth-century literature, as a political tool to demonstrate the Protestants' obligation to fight back. She piles example upon example in an attempt to capture the extent of the corruption and the dreadfulness of France's chaos. Tyranny is shown to reign unchecked, crime to prevail, justice to fail, and social order to collapse: "That is how these evil souls want to shake up heaven and earth, and by their malice overthrow piety and justice ..." (193). Particularly disturbing to Jeanne is the reversal of hierarchy: "the crown of our king half on the head of his enemy" (214). And again: "the glory of God we see every day trampled underfoot, and the blood of His elect spilled. The authority of his majesty was so disdained by these rebels who have broken his edicts and defied his commands that he no longer held the rank of king among them, and the princes of his royal blood were chased by foreign usurpers from the place they should possess." (213)

Both the Sorbonne and the Guises were held responsible by Protestants for their persecution. Besides offering a means of channeling their hatred, blaming specific individuals like the king's evil advisors, rather than blaming the king himself, had the advantage of allowing for the possibility of reconciliation with the crown.[63] A striking aspect of the style of the *Ample Declaration* is, on one hand, the unavoidable flattery used to evoke the king and the royal family and, on the other, the straightforwardness of the language when it refers to Jeanne's enemies. Here, the language is not merely direct, it is provocative and uncompromising. The Guises are accused of crimes of all sorts, such as taking advantage of the inexperience and kindness of the young king to usurp and abuse his authority (176). While the king whose reputation has been blackened because of his counselors' evil machinations is made to appear a marionnette in their hands, they emerge as exploiters of credulity (194), liars (228, 232), traitors (209), usurpers (176), murderers (175), and tyrants whose ultimate goal is to eradicate the True Religion (186).

Again and again undertones of indignation break through, most vividly in personal attacks. Although the Guises receive bad press throughout the *Ample Declaration*, the Cardinal de Lorraine in particular is by far Jeanne's favorite

---

62. Sara K. Barker, *Protestantism, Poetry and Protest: The Vernacular Writings of Antoine de Chandieu, c. 1534–1591* (Aldershot, UK: Ashgate, 2009), 159.

63. See Racaut, *Hatred in Print*, 71.

target. She goes to great lengths to destroy his credibility. The multiplication of strong derogatory terms reveals the intensity of her hatred and indignation. The terms "cruelty" usually contrasted with "his majesty's goodness" (195), "treason," "treachery," and "malice," used over and over again and accompanied by even more pejorative adjectives like "loathsome," "deceitful," "barbaric," sum up his character as a "bloodthirsty person" (180).

In her attempt to discredit the Cardinal de Lorraine, Jeanne also employs a variety of images. Three in particular express with striking vividness her hatred and disgust for him. These images are drawn from animal imagery, frequently used in polemical literature and by Calvin himself:[64] "how many cunning ruses he and his brother [the cardinal and the duc de Guise] employed" (174). In this particular case, Jeanne does not use the name of the fox but a derivative adjective ("renardes" translated as cunning), which gives the impression that the individual she describes is not *like* the animal, but that he *is* truly the animal because of specific traits he shares with it. In the Middle Ages, each vice had its corresponding animal. For hypocrisy, there was the fox. Even though the fox was well known to folk wisdom as the personification of deceit, Jeanne judges it important to describe the behavioral manifestations of this vice, as if she wanted everyone to know it when confronted by it. Like David who feels that he should warn the innocent, Jeanne makes it her duty to give cues that will allow the king and queen and the French people to see through deceitful appearances: "Anyone who has observed the cardinal's facial expressions has seen him feign so naturally kindness, misery and lassitude. The royal prophet, having encountered similar hypocrites, wanted to mark them so that they would be recognized by all" (174–75). Beyond the obvious centrality of the psalms in Protestant theology, Jeanne refers specifically to Psalm 10, a portrait of hypocrisy to strengthen her argument and justify the strong emphasis she places on this particular vice. Yet one cannot help wondering if Jeanne had another reason to refer to the Bible. Viewed through the biblical lens, denigration (the invective against the cardinal) is made to appear as serving a most laudable purpose, that of protecting the innocent against those who may try to abuse them.

Another animal that Jeanne evokes when she refers to the Cardinal de Lorraine is the crocodile : "O how many crocodile tears this cardinal shed" (174). This time, she employs a colloquial expression (to shed crocodile tears) so that all will see through the cardinal's deceit. But, most likely, the sixteenth-century reader saw beyond the surface an allusion to Satan (Satan was sometimes represented as a crocodile instead of a serpent) or, rather, a parallel between the deceitful demeanor of the cardinal and demonic temptation. This reading is corroborated by the words Jeanne uses elsewhere to describe the cardinal and various images throughout the *Ample Declaration*. When she refers to the Guises, for example,

---

64. See Francis M Higman, *The Style of John Calvin in his French Polemical Treatises* (Oxford: Oxford University Press, 1967), 146–52.

she frequently speaks of "their damnable ways" (179), and the cardinal is depicted as "this wretched and damnable cardinal" (195). Another reference to Satan, but this time as a snake, can be found in the image, repeated many times, of the cardinal spitting up his poisonous venom: "the venomous malice of the Cardinal de Lorraine" (199); "poison the mind of our young, naturally good king with their venomous temperament" (193).

Crocodiles are generally regarded as monstrous beasts. The emphasis on the cardinal's monstrosity can also be found in the image of vicious, hybrid creatures like the Hydra of Lerna: "the machinations of this Hydra; for every wicked head of his that one cuts off, seven more appear" (212). In the 1569 poem by Ronsard entitled *L'Hydre desfaict*, this motif serves to celebrate the duc d'Anjou's triumph at Jarnac and Montcontour. The heroic nature of his deed is underscored by the parallel established between the duke coming to the aid of his brother Charles IX in order to save the kingdom of France and Hercules slaying the Hydra. A recurrent motif in Renaissance literature and painting, the triumph of Hercules over the Lernaean Hydra typically stood as a political allegory of resistance to tyranny. Here, the emphasis is not placed on the exploit, but on the Hydra's monstrous power to produce evil over and over, which would leave its opponent with little hope for a successful outcome if God did not miraculously intervene. Jeanne cautions her enemies with the warning that, in the end, God's mercy will prevail, the innocent will be avenged by the righteous Judge, and the Hydra will be defeated: "But, in the end, he will find that God, the just judge, is his Hercules" (212).

Most striking are the passages where Jeanne shifts from argument to emotional appeal. These are generally filled with images in order to create vivid visualization that can provoke strong emotions: sympathy for "the hearts of all his faithful subjects [that] bleed with grief" (195) or the ship caught in a storm with no one capable of taking control of the steering to lead her to safety (209); pity for "those of the Religion … on the edge of despair because of it, both noble and commoner wandering in the fields, unable to return to their homes" (210); anger at the thought that "our foes, so cruel and savage that they did not distinguish between the noble and the commoner, sparing no one regardless of rank, age, or sex" (220); outrage at the sight of the Protestant "army" made of expectant mothers and suckling babes (212). This frightful spectacle is evoked not just for us to see, but also to hear. In place of the forceful sound of trumpets that one associates with a powerful army, we are made to hear the pitiful lament of the innocent (212).

On three occasions, Jeanne evokes her own tragedy, calling attention to her enemies' harshness in forcefully taking her only son away from her. The wife bereft of her husband, or the mother of her child, were topoi frequently used by both sides of the confessional divide. This emotional appeal to public sympathy is undoubtedly a powerful and effective tactic, especially when the mother herself, aware of the danger she faces, confesses her secret fear: "Tears came to my eyes at the thought of being separated from my children" (220). Through repetition (see 205 and 208), the image of the mother bereft of her children gains in force and persuasiveness.

If Jeanne plays on the tone, imagery, and style of polemic pamphlets in her *Ample Declaration* and has her text printed in a small and relatively inexpensive format that would facilitate a wide distribution, she does not seek to hide her identity, as writers of pamphlets often did. Hers is an open declaration, made by a well known public figure. Her claims of truth thus rest in part on her rank and reputation. Even the title foregoes the typically provocative titles of propagandistic pamphlets to foreground the author herself. Jeanne wrote most of the *Ample Declaration* in the first-person voice. Strikingly, however, both the introduction and the final sentences are written from the perspective of the third person. These passages paradoxically create a distance from Jeanne's political persona, but elucidate a more personal perspective, that of an individual conscience and that of a woman writer.

The Ample Declaration *and Sixteenth-Century Memoirs*

The term *mémoire*, the French "memoir," originally designated information such as financial records and family registries recorded for use in a judicial case. In the sixteenth century, the meaning of the term was extended to include a new genre in which an individual, in general of noble origin and out of favor with the reigning power, provides a personal account of events that occurred in his or her life. The writing of memoirs in early modern France was largely the province of men, but there were a few notable exceptions: in addition to Jeanne d'Albret, Charlotte Duplessis-Mornay (1550–1606) and Marguerite de Valois (1553–1615) both penned memoirs. The memoirist aimed either to bring to light certain truths by relating events personally witnessed or to inform posterity of an injustice committed against the author. Jeanne writes with both objectives in mind:

> If I described this injurious injustice more fully than the others, it is because not everyone who reads this will know the truth of the situation, and because this is the injustice that caused me the most grief. (191)

A close link therefore clearly exists, and has always existed, between the memorializing function and the judicial sphere.[65] They share the same context (the trial), subject material (the narration of a life, the narration of witnessed events), discursive modalities (vows/denials, accusations/protestations) and the same underlying principles (truth/falsehood, justice/injustice).

65. Nadine Kuperty-Tsur asserts that "Le mémorialiste présente son apologie comme un plaidoyer." See Kuperty-Tsur, *Se dire à la Renaissance: Les mémoires au XVIe siècle* (Paris: J. Vrin, 1997), 26.

The *Ample Declaration* includes many elements that identify it as belonging to this emerging genre of the memoir. In the place of the truth that is typically sworn at the beginning of a trial or the veracity claim found at the head of a memoir, Jeanne begins her text with a declaration of her moral responsibility: "I have always considered that if you are not inwardly satisfied with yourself, the satisfaction that others might have in you will only halfway soothe your conscience" (172–73). This test of sincerity is echoed by the penultimate sentence of the *Ample Declaration*, where Jeanne again insists on the truth of her text:

> I beseech those who read this to excuse the style of a woman, who considered so worthy the subject of her book that it did not require beguiling words to embellish it, only the truth which she observed so faithfully. (238)

The title under which Jeanne's text was printed—*Ample Declaration*—and the structuring principle of the entire text further frame Jeanne's work as a defense in response to indictments made against the Reformed party and against her in particular. Jeanne defends herself from a position of disgrace, a situation nearly universal among memoirists.[66] Berriot-Salvadore explains that Jeanne found herself "in the most precarious position imaginable, that of a queen who abandoned her subjects, and a mother who prematurely installed her son in the perilous role of leader of rebel armies."[67]

As the word *declaration* implies, Jeanne writes to raise her arguments, to clarify and to explain them. And in so doing she expands (or amplifies) the letters she had previously written. What results is an accumulation of evidence meant to justify the "Christian endeavor" (215) in general and her own political acts and decisions. The *Ample Declaration* seeks above all to exonerate Jeanne and the French Protestants of the accusations of treason and rebellion that the Catholic propaganda leveled at them. In addition to the protestations of loyalty that punctuate the text, Jeanne also lists the many services she has rendered the crown and underlines their significance. At times Jeanne denies a charge by directing it at her enemies instead:

> … are not the true rebels those who violate the king's ordinances, and those who wish to overthrow his edicts, massacre his people, conspire with foreign countries for their own profit, and seek to exterminate

---

66. Kuperty-Tsur asserts that "Presque tous les mémorialistes ont été victimes d'une disgrâce venue briser net une carrière jusque là glorieuse." *Se dire à la Renaissance*, 151.

67. Berriot-Salvadore, *Les femmes*, 391: "dans une situation la plus précaire qui soit, celle d'une reine qui a abandonné ses sujets, celle d'une mère qui, prématurément, fait de son fils le chef exposé des armées rebelles."

the princes of the blood and faithful officers of the crown in order to
execute more freely their evil deeds? (197–98)

In the *Ample Declaration*, Jeanne alternates perspectives, sometimes adopt-
ing the viewpoint of an eyewitness,[68] sometimes voicing what she considers common knowledge. In all cases, she presents herself as someone well-informed of
the religio-political situation and fully aware of its political and personal stakes.
Jeanne relates, for example, specific exchanges she had with Catherine de' Medici
as well as humiliations she suffered personally. For these parts of her narrative, she
evokes others who could support her testimony, as when she calls upon Monluc
as a witness: "Monluc knows how many times I prevented our people from assembling first" (208). At times, Jeanne suggests that Catherine de' Medici herself
will authenticate her account:

> I deem her a princess so virtuous and honest that she will always ac-
> knowledge that particular service, as will the person who told me so
> on her behalf (which she later confirmed to me personally), Brandon
> the messenger, and the others who received the message and the let-
> ter of credence from me. (182–83)

She also, unsurprisingly, turns to God: "as God is my witness" (196).

Jeanne claims that her personal knowledge is useful in establishing the
truth: "It may seem superfluous to speak about my own affairs, nonetheless, to
make known to everyone the long-standing malice of the Cardinal de Lorraine
and his brother the Sieur de Guise, I will say […]" (185–86). In order to vouch
for her statements personally, she limits her narrative to incidents she has experienced. As a result, she declines to provide details about Condé or the royal family, for example, instead bringing the narrative back to her own story: "I will not
expand on the voyage of the court, since others have written about it, and instead
will recount my own" (183).

At other moments, however, Jeanne evokes very public events as evidence
to substantiate her claims. When she states, for example, that "everyone knows
how much I wanted peace," (199) and that "[e]veryone knows that the Guises and
their followers were pursuing the death of the late king my husband," (175) she
suggests that her own perspective is simply representative of one shared by the
majority of sincere and loyal French subjects.

Criticism of those in power is another common trait in memoirs. Though
Jeanne never directly accuses the king or the queen mother, she condemns those
who act in their name and in their stead, thus implicitly criticizing the king for his
weakness, his credulity, and his inability to control the situation in France:

68. On the memoirist's role as eyewitness see Kuperty-Tsur, *Se dire à la Renaissance*, 134.

> I finally came to the realization, to my great regret, that the king-
> dom's affairs were on the verge of ruin. Instead of taking good and
> prompt measures, based on counsel received daily from their most
> loyal subjects, their majesties allowed the enemies of the kingdom to
> batter its foundation through their crimes and their challenges to the
> king's very authority in his edicts. (208–9)

And elsewhere: "Or their majesties would become hardened by evil and abandon the helm of this poor kingdom to the winds and tides of adversity in the hands of its traitorous pilots, in whom they place too much trust" (209). Jeanne's narrative, along with those of her ally, the Prince de Condé, and her archenemy, Blaise de Monluc, provide readers with a rare glimpse into the legal, political and personal arenas of the French Wars of Religion.

In the last lines of what is in part a justificatory memoir, Jeanne apologizes for her plain "style of a woman" (238). Placed in the prefaces of women's writings, this conventional humility topos typically serves to legitimize their foray into the male-dominated sphere of writing. As a concluding statement, the confession of weakness paradoxically becomes a defense of women's writing. Jeanne aligns the plain style of a woman with the "truth she so faithfully observed" (238) and contrasts it with ornate rhetoric of men which she sees as deceitful ("beguiling words," 238).[69] The association of truth with plain style leads to a reconsideration of her detractors' derogatory remarks about her as a feebleminded woman. In this context and in light of previous passages such as that one where Jeanne evokes the little dog used by God to confound the powerful (187) or the one where she refers to her own "simplicity" that makes her dependent on God (217), the accusation of female imbecility takes on a new spiritual meaning. Female ignorance (which is another facet of female humility) echoes a Reformed paradigm that infuses the *Ample Declaration* and suggests that Jeanne, as one of the wise fools (God's elect),[70] has been charged with a divine mission.

Jeanne's remarkable strategies of reversal demonstrate her mastery of rheto-ric and the power of the plain "style of a woman." Simply by displacing it, Jeanne

---

69. See also the prologue of Marguerite de Navarre's *Heptameron* where Jeanne's mother makes a similar juxtaposition between male rhetoric and female truth (trans. P. A. Chilton, London: Penguin Books, 1984, 68–9). Kuperty-Tsur argues that the rejection of ornate rhetoric by late sixteenth-cen-tury memoirists corresponds to a rejection of the mannerist style associated with those in power: "Justice historique et écriture mémorialiste," in *Écriture de soi et argumentation, rhétorique et modèles de l'autoreprésentation: Actes du colloque de l'Université de Tel-Aviv, 3–5 mai 1998*, ed. Kuperty-Tsur (Caen: Presses universitaires de Caen, 2000), 60.

70. This, too, constitutes a common theme in Marguerite de Navarre's evangelical theater (see the characters of the *Ravie* in the *Comédie de Mont-de-Marsan*, the chambermaid in *Le Mallade*, and the children in *L'Inquisiteur*). In *Théâtre de femmes de l'ancien régime*, v.1 XVIᵉ siècle, ed. Catherine Masson and Nancy Erickson Bouzrara (Saint Étienne: Publications de l'Université de Saint Étienne, 2006).

turns a prefatory topos into a defense of women's writing and transforms her adversaries' invective into a tool of female empowerment.

The Afterlife of the Ample Declaration

The *Ample Declaration* was printed in La Rochelle three times (two editions in 1569 and one in 1570 as part of the *Histoire de nostre temps*) by Barthélemy Berton, the primary printer of propaganda for the French Protestant leaders during the Third War of Religion.[71] Fewer than thirty copies still exist[72] since, like many small, inexpensive books at the time, the *Ample Declaration* was a topical text, not intended to survive as a collector's item. As Andrew Pettegree reminds us, "overall less than one per cent of the total copies of books printed in the sixteenth century have survived to the present day. For pamphlets the figure is even lower."[73]

Moreover, the propagandistic content of the *Ample Declaration* rendered its existence unwelcome in a France trying to recover from the Wars of Religion through a policy of benign repression of painful memories. Further, the combative Jeanne d'Albret was overshadowed by the conciliatory figure of her son, Henri IV, to the extent that her rediscovery would wait until the nineteenth century when the Baron de Ruble brought new attention to her life and works. In 1893 he published a modern French edition of the *Ample Declaration* under the title *Mémoires et poésies de Jeanne d'Albret*.[74] As part of a more recent interest in the history of the Reformation and the writings of early modern women, Bernard Berdou d'Aas published a French edition in 2007 including two versions, one that reproduced the 1570 edition and one with modernized spelling.[75] We are aware of no complete English translation of the *Ample Declaration* that predates the present translation.

---

71. For more on the material production of the book, see Eugénie Droz, *Barthélemy Berton, 1563–1573* (Geneva: Droz, 1960).

72. See the Universal Short Title Catalogue for details: <http://ustc.ac.uk>.

73. Andrew Pettegree, *The Book in the Renaissance* (New Haven and London: Yale University Press, 2010), 334.

74. Jeanne d'Albret, *Mémoires et poésies*, ed. Alphonse de Ruble (Paris: Libraires de la Bibliothèque Nationale, 1893).

75. Jeanne d'Albret, *Lettres: suivies d'une Ample Déclaration*, ed. Bernard Berdou d'Aas (Biarritz: Atlantica, 2007).

A Note on the Translation

The texts presented here are translated from the 1570 edition of the *Ample Declaration* reprinted in *Histoire de nostre temps, contenant un recueil des choses mémorables passées & publiées pour le faict de la religion & estat de la France depuis l'edict de pacification du 23 Jour de mars, jusqu'au present (The History of our time containing a collection of memorable things that happened in the past and were published pertaining to religion and the state of France from the Edict of Pacification of March 23rd to the present)*. Our primary objective has been comprehensibility and readability while bringing the twenty-first century reader as close as reasonably possible to the experience of reading the original text. Hence the emphasis placed here on preserving the stylistic properties and vocabulary of the original.

By far the most challenging aspect of Jeanne's sixteenth-century prose has been her very long sentences containing "the grafting of subsequent, often unrelated, thoughts to previous ones."[1] This formal style, still heavily influenced by the habits of an oral culture, is not only off-putting to modern readers used to written texts with distinct, individual sentences, but often suggests confusing semantic causalities. We thus have chosen to cut these sentences into independently significant shorter sentences, but in so doing we had to decide when to retain the notion of causality and when to make a more complete break.

We have made every effort to retain the intricacies of Jeanne's language, indicative of the complexity of her situation and motives. However, as translation inevitably requires interpretation, we have clarified some awkward and unclear passages at the possible expense of intentional ambiguities. As would be required in any translation from French to English, we altered the order of words so as to respect proper English syntax. In some cases we modified the word order to foreground meaningful parallelism.

A grammatical property of early modern texts is vague pronoun references. There are also various moments where Jeanne is not clear about the person or persons to whom she is referring, such as when she uses the pronoun *ils* to refer to the Guises or the enemies of the Protestants, or when the pronoun used shifts from singular to plural without explanation. To avoid confusion, pronouns have sometimes been replaced by proper names.

We have attempted to remain true to some degree to the flavor of the language of the period. French titles like sieur, lieutenant général, maître de requêtes have been preserved in French. Blatantly anachronistic words or phrases have been eschewed, and a few archaisms have been allowed. However, when such words would have required an explanatory note, rather than adding another layer

---

1. Neuschel, *Word of Honor,* 104.

of interpretation and distracting readers from the text, they have been either modernized or retained in French.

"Doublets" (the use of pairs of synonymous nouns or adjectives, such as *miseres et calamitez, opprimée et affligée*) were a characteristic feature of sixteenth-century French. We have chosen to render them in the following ways:

1. If the repetition in and of itself was judged to convey semantic emphasis, we retained both terms.
2. If the terms appeared merely redundant, we have translated them with a single word.
3. If the terms carried different nuances, we have either preserved the pairs as such or replaced two nouns with the more common English combination of adjective and noun or replaced two adjectives with one adjective modified by an adverb.

We have followed similar reasoning for "triplets."

Letters from the queen of Navarre to the king, to the queen his mother,
to Monsieur brother of the king, to Monsieur le Cardinal de Bourbon
her brother-in-law, and to the queen of England

Accompanied by an Ample Declaration, an extended explanation of these letters,[1]
containing the reasons
for her departure with Monseigneur le Prince and Madame
Catherine, her children, to join the general cause with Monseigneur
le Prince de Condé, her brother-in-law

---

1. The 1570 edition of the *Histoire de notre temps* includes a letter "written at court by the agent of the Cardinal de Crequy, to his master 9 August 1568." As Jeanne did not write the letter herself and as its authenticity is difficult to ascertain, it is not included here.

To the king[2]

Monseigneur, when the Sieur de La Mothe[3] delivered your letter to me, I was already well along on my journey, having been compelled to leave by a change that had been threatening us for some time. [158] The animosity of our enemies seemed to us so extreme that their passionate fury smothered the hope for peace offered by your Edict of Pacification,[4] Monseigneur, which was not only hardly observed, but entirely overturned by the Cardinal de Lorraine's ruses.[5] In spite of the promises it pleased you to make to all your wretched subjects of the Reformed faith, the Cardinal de Lorraine has rendered the Edict useless by continually blocking its implementation (writing letters to the parlements as well as others, of which I am well aware in the case of Guyenne). While keeping everything unsettled, he had many massacres carried out. Because we endured his strange ways he felt emboldened to set his sights on the princes of your blood,[6] as exemplified by his pursuit of Monsieur le Prince my brother,[7] who was forced to seek help among his relations.[8] He is so tightly allied to me and so close to my son that we could do no less, Monseigneur, than to offer him that which blood ties and friendship require of us. We are well aware of your will; you have abundantly conveyed to us in spoken and written words that you wish us to serve you with all the loyalty, obedience, and reverence we owe you, and we will never fail to do so for as long as we live. And we are even more certain that out of your goodness and natural affection toward us [159] you seek our preservation, not our ruin. Considering

2. Charles Maximilien (1550–1574), third son of Henri II and Catherine de' Medici, became king of France as Charles IX upon the death of his brother François II in 1560. He was king during the massacre of Huguenot leaders assembled in Paris on the occasion of Marguerite de Valois's (his sister) wedding to Henri de Navarre, the future King Henri IV.

3. Bertrand de Salignac Fénelon, seigneur de la Mothe (1523–1589), French diplomat. He served as French ambassador to England from 1568–1575.

4. The Edict of Longjumeau, signed by Charles IX and Catherine de' Medici on March 23, 1568, brought the second civil war to an end.

5. Charles de Guise de Lorraine (1524–1574), second son of Claude de Guise and Antoinette de Bourbon, brother of François, second duc de Guise, named Cardinal de Guise in 1547. Protestant pamphlets of the time denigrated him for his duplicity and ruthlessness and held him personally responsible for the persecution of the Huguenots. In her *Ample Declaration*, Jeanne employs numerous images to denounce what she sees as his despicable character; see for example 174–75.

6. The Bourbons to whom Jeanne refers here (see next note) were "a branch of the house of Capet, which constituted the so-called third race of France's kings." See Michael Wolfe, "Bourbon Family and Dynasty," in Paul F. Grendler, ed., *Encyclopedia of the Renaissance* (New York: Charles Scribner's Sons, 1999), 1:268.

7. See Introduction, note 11.

8. A reference to the plot to capture Condé in Burgundy. According to Jeanne, the Cardinal de Lorraine was the instigator of that plot.

such efforts directed against us, who would not judge that they are carried out without your knowledge by the notoriously malicious Cardinal de Lorraine? For we all know that you are a truthful king and that you promised us something quite different. For you, I will explain what we are truly doing, since we already know.

I therefore very humbly beseech you, my Lord, to look kindly upon my leaving home with my son, with the intention of serving my God, you, my sovereign king, and my family. We will oppose, as long as we have life and means, the endeavors of those who overtly and maliciously intend to do violence to you. Please believe, Monseigneur, that we carry arms only for these three reasons: to prevent our enemies from eliminating us from the face of the earth, as they plotted,[9] and to serve you, and to protect the princes of your blood. The cardinal wronged me, too, when he attempted to convert your power and authority into violent means and tried to wrest my son from my arms[10] in order to deliver him to you, as if your simple command did not have enough power over us. We very humbly beseech you, Monseigneur, to believe that we are your very humble and obedient servants, and that our loyalty is of equal measure to the disloyalty [160] of the cardinal and his accomplices. I assure you that when it pleases you to compare us both, you will find more truth in my actions than in his words, as the gentleman that I am sending to your majesties will confirm, as will Monsieur de La Mothe. He leaves, I am certain, satisfied with my intentions, which will always be to commit my life and possessions to the conservation of your greatness and your reign, upon which I beseech God to bestow his benediction as well as to give you, Monseigneur, a very long life.

From Bergerac, September 16, 1568
Your most humble and obedient subject and aunt,

Jane[11]

---

9. A reference to conspiracy theories inspired by the meeting in 1565 at Bayonne between Catherine de' Medici, Charles IX and the duke of Alva representing King Philip II. See Roelker, *Queen of Navarre*, 234.

10. A reference to the August 1568 plot to capture the young Henri, Jeanne's son, and take him back to court. Losses and Monluc with the aid of several Catholic seigneurs from Navarre were instrumental in that plot but again Jeanne blames exclusively the Cardinal de Lorraine. See Roelker, *Queen of Navarre*, 305.

11. This is not the editors' translation of Jeanne, but the way she wrote her name.

To the queen, my sovereign lady[12]

Madame, I will begin my letter with a declaration before God and man that there is nothing more absolute than the devotion that I had, have, and will have to the service of my God, my king, my country, and my lineage.[13] My devotion has inspired such strength in me that by the time Monsieur de La Mothe arrived at my estates, I had already left, prepared to offer up my life, my possessions, and all my resources. If you find my letter too long, Madame, I very humbly beseech you to attribute it to the necessities of the times, which [161] have charged me with responsibility upon responsibility, so that I am forced to clarify my intent for you, as briefly as possible. I open my heart to you so that you can read the opposite of the lies that the enemies[14] of God, the king, and therefore of his loyal subjects and serviteurs[15] will, I am certain, try to make you believe.

I again humbly beseech you, Madame, to pardon me if I begin my account at an earlier time in order to explain fully the state to which I have been reduced. I must begin when those of the house of Guise declared themselves enemies of the peace in this kingdom by their actions, when they bribed the late king my husband[16] with the false promise of regaining our kingdom.[17] You know well, Madame, who was manipulating him,[18] to my great regret and yours, if I dare say, as I had the honor, at that time, of hearing it from your own mouth. I very humbly beseech you to remember the loyalty you found in me when the conservation of the kingdom was at stake. I sacrificed the bond with a husband and risked losing my children. As for my possessions, since I was losing everything else, I do not wish

12. Catherine de' Medici (1519–1589), the queen mother and, between 1560 and 1563, regent of France.

13. Jeanne points out over and over again her sense of integrity, her strong faith, and her loyalty toward her king. The stance of good Christian and loyal subject becomes a leitmotiv in the *Ample Declaration*. This protestation of loyalty is typical of Reformed rhetoric after the Conspiracy of Amboise, when Protestants were represented in Catholic propaganda as rebels and enemies of the French crown. See Introduction, 32.

14. A reference to the Guises.

15. In order to bring attention to its multiple possible meanings, we have chosen not to translate the term serviteur. Although it can refer to a paid domestic worker (servant), Jeanne also uses it to refer to those who choose to put themselves in her service in exchange for patronage or protection (retainers).

16. Antoine de Bourbon (1518–1562), duc de Vendôme, later king of Navarre through his marriage to Jeanne. Jeanne goes to great lengths in her *Ample Declaration* (at 175–186) to describe the maneuvers that the Guises employed first to eliminate Antoine, then to win him to their side.

17. Antoine de Bourbon was obsessed with regaining parts of the kingdom of Navarre conquered by Ferdinand II of Aragon earlier in the century.

18. Jeanne is intimating that under the Guises' pressure, Antoine finally opted for the Catholic party. This led Antoine to consider repudiating the Protestant Jeanne and reinforced the power of the Guises at court. See Roelker, *Queen of Navarre*, 181.

to consider them here. I again very humbly beseech you, Madame, to recall the words it pleased you to address to me leaving Fontainebleau,[19] and the assurance you received from me, which, for my part, has not changed nor diminished with time. If it [162] pleases you, Madame, you will also remember that after arriving in Vendosmois, I received your letters and your orders, which I faithfully obeyed. Next I will describe what I did after my arrival in Guyenne, all in accordance with your wishes which it pleased you to convey to me through my maître d'hôtel Roques.[20] At that point, Madame, I lost the late king my husband,[21] and since then I have shared in the afflictions of widowhood. Since we are speaking of generalities, Madame, may God keep me from reminding you of the indignities that I have personally suffered.[22] For I declare a second time that the service to my God and my king, the love of my country and my lineage so fill my heart that there is no space for any personal passion of my own.

So, Madame, this brings me to the last war[23] which began when the Cardinal de Lorraine and his accomplices pushed us to the limits, as you and everyone else know. During this time I stayed in my lands, useless to the service of your majesties because I was unable to do what I wanted. Those evil men who restrained me then would have done the same to me this time, Madame, if they could have. The Sieur de La Mothe, whom you sent to me twice during that period, will have given you by now such an accurate description of my actions that I need not recount them again. [163] I thus turn, Madame, to my current situation: I have witnessed the edicts[24] of my king not only occasionally violated (which might have been excusable), but completely overturned, his authority scorned, his royal promises broken, and all this by the damnable, deceitful Cardinal de Lorraine. I cannot paint a truer picture than the one I know (and I truly know) and you, Madame, know him too. You have witnessed many sad consequences including

19. Antoine ordered Jeanne to leave Fontainebleau in late March 1562. See *Ample Declaration*, 181.

20. Jean de Secondat, seigneur de Roques.

21. Antoine de Bourbon died on November 17, 1562.

22. Several pages in the *Ample Declaration* are devoted to the description of the indignities suffered by Jeanne; see 187–94.

23. Many historians cite Condé's failed attempt to kidnap Charles IX at Meaux on September 29, 1567, as the start of the Second War of Religion.

24. The Edict of Saint-Germain, signed on January 15, 1562, authorized Huguenot worship in the private households of nobles and in the suburb of one town in each *sénéchaussée*. The Edict of Amboise, signed on March 19, 1563, ended the First War of Religion. It granted individual freedom of conscience in their own homes, but limited the right to preach to a few specific locations. Religious prisoners were to be released and property that had been confiscated, restored. The Edict of Longjumeau, issued on March 23, 1568, officially ended the Second War of Religion by restoring in full the religious privileges and freedoms that had been granted in the Edict of Amboise.

the massacres,[25] and your ears are still ringing with complaints about them. You have seen those who wander aimlessly through France,[26] cut off from their natural sustenance while soldiers eat their food, and who had hoped that the Edict of Pacification would allow them to return to a peaceful home. And what is worse, the Cardinal de Lorraine and his accomplices, emboldened by our endurance of their barbarous cruelty, have attacked the princes of the blood, branches of this tree that they wish to uproot, once they have stripped it of its branches.[27] They are not motivated by religious zeal, as they claim. When you were recently so ill[28] (may God always grant you good health, Madame) you know that Monsieur le Cardinal my brother[29] was not spared their conspiracies, even though he is Catholic. It is the blood of France that inflames their hearts with spite; see how they have pursued Monsieur le Prince, my brother,[30] and all his young children. We felt, my son and I, compelled to come to their aid because of our shared blood, and we did not want [164] to fail in any way to do this. I will not forget to mention Monsieur de Losse's[31] mission targeting my son. All of this was under the tyrannical counsel of the cardinal and his accomplices.

I know well, Madame, that those who hear my letter read will claim that I imitated letters that you received from all over, and that these words are not my own. I very humbly beseech you, Madame, to believe that when we of the Reformed faith speak of the sole subject that moves us, there can be only one way to express these grievances, just as, from a bloodline as illustrious as the Bourbon's, stem of the fleur de lis, there can only come loyalty. Hence, Madame, these are the three principles that motivated me: first, the service to my God, seeing all those who profess the true religion threatened to be wiped from the face of the earth by the cardinal and his accomplices (which is all too clear); secondly, the service to my king, for which I will use my life and possessions so that the Edict of

25. Massacres frequently mentioned in Protestant propaganda include: Vassy (March 1, 1562), Sens (April 12–14, 1562), Orange (June 6, 1562), and Tours (July 1562). The "Surprise of Meaux," a failed conspiracy organized by Condé in September 1567 to capture Charles IX and Catherine de' Medici, triggered new outbreaks of violence and the Second War of Religion. For analyses of religious violence see Natalie Zemon Davis, "The Rites of Violence: Religious Riot in Sixteenth-Century France," *Past & Present* 59, no. 1 (1973): 51–91, and Judith Pollman, "Countering the Reformation in France and the Netherlands: Clerical Leadership and Catholic Violence 1560–1585," *Past & Present* 190, no. 1 (2006): 83–120.

26. See *Ample Declaration*, 220–21.

27. Jeanne intimates that the Guises are attempting to take over the French crown at the expense of the Bourbon princes of the blood. Such an accusation is typical of the pamphlet literature of the 1560s.

28. In April 1568, Catherine de' Medici nearly died of a catarrh fever. Albret, *Mémoires et poésies*, 212n2, mentions two letters by Francis de Alava concerning the queen's illness.

29. She means her brother-in-law, the Cardinal Charles de Bourbon (1523–1590), a staunch Catholic.

30. She means her brother-in-law, the prince de Condé.

31. Jean de Baulieu, Sieur de Losses, a Catholic who had served as Henri de Navarre's tutor.

Pacification will be observed according to his will, and so that our France, mother of so many noble souls, will not be drained of her maternal milk and her children left to die; finally, our blood ties that call us, Madame, to offer all possible aid to Monsieur le Prince, my brother, who is obviously being pursued, against the king's will and despite his many guarantees of safety. His evil adversaries have too long assumed a place beside you and our king, a place to which they have no right. They cover your eyes [165] so that you do not see their malice, and block your ears so that you do not hear our grievances. May God, by his holy grace, uncover your eyes, Madame, and unblock your ears, so that you might see and hear with what zealous devotion each of us strives to conserve your majesties' grandeur, though we know well from the letter you sent through the Sieur de La Mothe how they turned you against us.

Madame, I am sending you one of my gentlemen along with the Sieur de La Mothe to confirm what I am writing. I spoke to him at length and asked him to tell you how necessary it is, among other things, that you detach yourself from those who aim to undermine your authority by trying to ruin those who want you to maintain it. Know us all well, distinguish those who are good from those who are evil, and believe, Madame, that I in particular profoundly desire a just peace, one so secure that the Cardinal de Lorraine and his supporters can no longer undermine it. If God had graced me with the ability to serve that peace, I would consider myself fortunate and willing to devote my life and all the rest to it.

Praying God, Madame, etc.
From Bergerac, September 16, 1568
Your most humble and obedient subject and sister,

Jane

[166]

To Monsieur, [brother of the king][32]

Monsieur, I know that second to the king,[33] you have such power that all your humble serviteurs, loyal subjects of his majesty, legitimately look to you to intervene in the stormy uproar that relentlessly batters our poor France. Those responsible for this evil have always sought to demolish France, wanting to

---

32. Henri (1551–1589), fourth son of Henri II and Catherine de' Medici, duc d'Anjou, Henri III of France (1575–1589).

33. Henri had been named lieutenant général de France after the death of the Constable Anne de Montmorency on November 12, 1567.

build their own dominance and authority by ruining the subjects who support her, like strong pillars. I fear deeply, Monsieur, that I will not be so fortunate that my words will reach you, that instead they will be diverted by the Cardinal de Lorraine. I know that he will, as much as he can, prevent the king, the queen, and you from being accurately informed of the misery and calamities that afflict France through his machinations, as shown by the letters he has dispersed in so many places. The only purpose of those letters is to overturn the edicts of his majesty and to massacre all those who want them observed. The latest actions, which he undertook to trap Monsieur le Prince my brother,[34] demonstrate that he is particularly targeting the princes of your blood. Monsieur le Prince, not wanting to be the first to break the peace, preferred to withdraw with his wife and small children.[35] With such cruelty on one side, and such piteousness on the other, I am certain, Monsieur, that if the truth [167] could be described to you as it really is, it would move your heart more because of the blood they have the honor of sharing with you. For this reason, my son and I set out to give them the aid that our close relations require of us, with the means that God has given us. I very humbly beseech you, Monsieur, to believe that wherever my son and I are, we will be there in the service of God and the king, whom we will continue to serve humbly and dutifully for our entire lives, as we will you. I present you, Monsieur, my most humble compliments. And since the Sieur de La Mothe will more amply explain all of this to you, I will end my letter, beseeching God to give you, Monsieur, a long and very happy life.

From Bergerac, September 16, 1568.
Your very humble and very obedient aunt,

Jeanne

To Monsieur my brother, Monsieur le Cardinal, etc.[36]

Monsieur my brother, the Sieur de La Mothe and a gentleman that I am sending with him will relate to their majesties, the circumstances that legitimately led me to where the Sieur de La Mothe found me, hoping to pursue [168] my voyage in their service, which you can also see in the letters that I wrote to them. It is time, Monsieur my brother, that you more boldly inform them of the extreme suffering of our France. If all the king's subjects are obliged to inform him, is not more

34. On this plot to capture the Prince de Condé, Jeanne's brother-in-law, see above, note 8.

35. Jeanne's recourse to pathos with the reference to Condé's spouse and young children also forced to take flight is carried much further in the *Ample Declaration*; see below, 69–70.

36. Here and below she means her brother-in-law, Charles de Bourbon.

expected of you who are also obliged to do so by the honor of your blood?[37] Will the Cardinal de Lorraine always have you as a subordinate? Will he shame you by wronging your own brother, sisters, and nephews without your even wanting revenge? If you do not do it for us, your close relations, and if you do not wish to take up the quarrel for reasons of religion (as the cardinal hides behind religious zeal), at least remember the Sicilian Vespers[38] that he and his accomplices plotted when the queen was recently so ill. You were distressed about it and lost sleep over it for one night, but then all that concern went up in smoke. The cardinal deluded you with his honeyed words. If religion divides us, can our blood ties be severed for that cause?[39] Will friendship and innate duty cease for this reason? No, Monsieur my brother. I beseech you, avenge the pursuit of our brother[40] to show that my son is wronged by it, and acknowledge for my sake the honor of the house[41] into which I married, and the one that I consider my own. We will devote ourselves to this house, faithfully offering all the service, obedience, and loyalty that we owe [169] our king. And because, Monsieur, the occupation of women and of those like you who do not carry arms is to strive for peace,[42] do your part to ensure that we succeed. As for me, I will use all possible means to this end. And know that three things lead my son and me here: God, the king, and our lineage, all three of which we eagerly serve. The Sieur de La Mothe will tell you how things develop, and I pray God, Monsieur my brother, that He bestow upon you His holy grace, etc.

From Bergerac, September 16, 1568
Your obedient and beholden sister,

Jane

37. Jeanne begins by appealing to Charles's sense of duty. She claims that it is his duty as a first prince of the blood to counsel the king.

38. A comparison between a violent revolt against French royal authority in thirteenth-century Sicily and a supposed plot by the Guises to assassinate the Cardinal de Bourbon.

39. Jeanne now appeals to Charles's sense of family. Here she intimates that blood ties are stronger than religious convictions.

40. The Prince de Condé was forced to flee to La Rochelle; see *Ample Declaration*, see below, 69.

41. Jeanne here appeals to Charles's sense of rank, for he belongs to the house of Bourbon and as such is a prince of the blood.

42. Jeanne argues that women's business is to make peace, a role that would have seemed appropriate for woman at the time but also that the queen herself had judged appropriate for Jeanne. In her *Ample Declaration* (199), Jeanne says that it was under such pretense that she had been lured back to court. This role of conciliator had the potential to give women a powerful role within the family and in society. Louise de Savoie, mother of François I, Margaret of Austria, Regent of the Netherlands and Charles's aunt, and Marguerite de Navarre, François's sister and Jeanne's mother played such a role when they negotiated the "Paix des Dames" (the Ladies' Peace) of 1529, which ended one phase of the hostilities between François I and Charles V of Habsburg, Holy Roman Emperor.

To the queen of England[43]

Madame, above and beyond the desire that I have had my entire life to remain in your good graces, I would be guilty of a grave omission if I did not explain in my letters to you the reason that brought me here today, with the two children with whom God has blessed me.[44] My offense would be all the more serious, considering that God in his great goodness filled you with such virtues and zeal for the advancement of his glory and chose you to be one of the nurturing queens of his church.[45] It is right and just, then, that all those, united through this cause, join you [170] in your saintly mission and inform you about what is happening in this regard.

Since I am certain that you are well aware of the overall situation, Madame, I will address my own particular circumstances. I very humbly beseech you to believe that three things (the least of which would have sufficed) led me to leave my kingdom and sovereign countries. The first is the Reformed faith, grievously suppressed in our France by the ever barbaric Cardinal de Lorraine, seconded by men of the same persuasion as he. I would have been ashamed that my name was ever included among the faithful, had I not dedicated all the means that God gave me to opposing such heresy and horror and had we, my son and I, not joined such great and holy princes and seigneurs. Like them, I have resolved with the grace of the great God of hosts[46] to spare neither blood, nor life, nor possessions for this purpose. The second thing, Madame, bound with the first, is the service to our king, for the ruin of the Church is also his ruin and that of his kingdom, the strength and grandeur of which we must strictly preserve. And because my son and I have the honor of being among his closest relations, Madame, we hastened to oppose those who made the king the author of his own ruin by taking advantage of his great benevolence [171]. Although he is the most truthful prince in the world, they prevented him from keeping his promises when they conspired to undo the Edict of Pacification.[47] When respected in its entirety, that edict

43. Elizabeth I (1533–1603), daughter of Henry VIII and Anne Boleyn, and queen of England (1558–1603). Although she supported the French leaders of the Reformation as a fellow Protestant, she was careful to maintain good diplomatic relations with the French royal family at the same time.

44. Jeanne also had a daughter, Catherine de Bourbon (1559–1604), princess of the blood, who championed the Reformation and the rights of Huguenots at court after her brother, Henri IV, abjured the Protestant faith in 1593. See Roelker, *Queen of Navarre*, 410–48 and "The Appeal of Calvinism to French Noblewomen," 403.

45. At the beginning of her reign, she restored the Protestant religion in England and allowed the repatriation of the Protestant leaders who had been expelled by Mary Tudor.

46. An expression frequently used in the Old Testament (see for example Isaiah 22:12) to designate God's omnipotence while pointing out the sacred responsibility of the people of Israel to fight for, and conquer the land of their heritage.

47. See above, note 4.

maintained peace between the king and his loyal subjects, and when disobeyed, it turned this loyalty into an obligation that violently forced each of us, against our will, into a wretched war.

The third thing, Madame, is particular to my son and me. We saw the enemies of God and of our ancestors, driven by their manifest hatred for us combined with the hatred they bear the general cause, resolve to destroy our lineage with a shameless and devastating hostility. We saw Monsieur le Prince de Condé, my brother, rather than taking up arms to avoid the plot against him, reduced instead to seeking a safe haven for his family. I tell you, Madame, the spectacle of these princes, in their tender youth, fleeing with their pregnant mother, was so piteous that no one with a good heart could remain untouched upon hearing of it. For my part, I was warned that someone had been sent to wrest my son from my very arms. Facing such a situation, we could do nothing less than come together, to live or to die united, as the shared blood that brought us to this point obliges us.

There you see [172], Madame, the three reasons that made me do what I have done, and take up arms. It is not against the heavens that these arms have been directed, as good Catholics claim, Madame, and even less against our king. We are not, by the grace of God, guilty of divine or human lèse-majesté. I very humbly beseech you to continue to provide us with your favor, trusting that we are faithful to our God and our king. May God acknowledge the favor you show us and grant you all heavenly benedictions and the conservation of your offices and estates. May it please you, Madame, to receive the very humble recommendations of the mother and her children, who profoundly wish to find means to be of service to you. And because, Madame, the Sieur du Chastelier,[48] lieutenant général of the Navy, who will always enjoy your favor, is traveling your way, I have asked him to present my letters to you, and I dare presume to recommend him to you.

From La Rochelle, October 16, 1568.
From your very humble and obedient sister,

Jane

---

48. Chastelier-Portaut, seigneur de la Tour, was sent to England in October 1568 for support and munitions. See Albret, *Mémoires et poésies*, 221n1.

Ample Declaration[49] of the preceding letters

[172] I have always considered that if you are not inwardly satisfied with yourself, the satisfaction that [173] others might have in you will only halfway soothe your conscience.[50] In the several letters that I wrote to his majesty the king,[51] to the queen mother,[52] to Monsieur the king's brother,[53] and to Monsieur the Cardinal de Bourbon, my brother-in-law,[54] and later to the queen of England,[55] I only briefly mentioned matters that I wish to make everyone understand more fully. I there-fore took quill in hand to elaborate upon the principal subject in these letters, that is to say, the circumstances that forced me to abandon my sovereign lands.[56] And because my intention is to explain in more detail those motivations that I only outlined in my letters, which are faith, service to his majesty the king, and duty to lineage, I will begin with faith.

Since the year 1560, there is no one unaware that it pleased the Lord to extricate me by his grace from the idolatry in which I was deeply mired, and to receive me into his church.[57] From then on, he helped me, by his same grace, persevere in his church and ever since I have devoted myself to the promotion of the Reformed cause. Even during the time of the late king my husband,[58] whose retreat from his initial zeal for the faith,[59] was a painful thorn, not in my side,

49. The title that is already familiar to readers is retained, but this declaration is understood to be an extended explanation of the letters.

50. This opening statement, all the more striking in a woman's text, is indicative of Jeanne d'Albret's strong sense of self, of Protestant rhetoric, and of the general tone of the memoir. See Eugénie Pascal, "*Lettres de la Royne de Navarre ... avec une Ample Declaration d'icelles*: autoportrait d'une femme d'exception," in *Jeanne d'Albret et sa cour : Actes du colloque international de Pau 17–19 mai 2001*, ed. Évelyne Berriot-Salvadore, Philippe Chareyre, and Claudie Martin-Ulrich (Paris: Honoré Champion, 2004), 257.

51. Charles IX (1550–1574), third son of Henri II and Catherine de' Medici, king of France 1561–1574.

52. Catherine de' Medici.

53. Henri, duc d'Anjou, future King Henri III.

54. Charles, Cardinal de Bourbon.

55. Elizabeth I.

56. A reference to her escape from Béarn, September, 6, 1568, and to the journey to La Rochelle where she arrived September 28, 1568. It was there that she wrote the *Ample Declaration*.

57. According to Jeanne d'Albret's historiographer, Nicolas de Bordenave, she attended the Reformed service in Pau (Béarn) and publicly adjured Catholicism on Christmas day 1560: Bordenave, *Histoire de Béarn et Navarre*, 108. She immediately forwarded the news of her conversion to Théodore de Bèze in Geneva. On Bèze, see Introduction, note 27. See Roelker, *Queen of Navarre*, 151–54 and Bryson, *Queen Jeanne*, 108–17, on possible religious and political motivations for Jeanne's conversion.

58. Antoine de Bourbon (1518–1562), duc de Vendôme, and *jure uxoris* king of Navarre (1555–1562).

59. After the Edict of January (1562), Antoine de Bourbon opted openly for Catholicism. Until then, he had vacillated between one side and the other, trying to use his equivocal position to attain territorial

but in my heart. Everyone knows (and it is more fitting that I keep silent rather than to say more) that neither his favor nor his harshness[60] moved me [174] in one direction or another. By the grace of God I have always followed the path of righteousness.[61] I will say, furthermore, that among so many assaults, my son was kept in the purity of his faith[62] by this same, and I will add, miraculous, grace. This did not occur through prudence, strength or steadfastness on my son's part, for at the age of eight, he could not yet have been equipped with those qualities; all the glory is due to God alone. And because, in the letter that I wrote to the queen, I reminded her of the time when those of the House of Guise and others encroached upon the rights of the late king my husband, I wish all to understand that by feeding his hopes to regain our kingdom,[63] and by deceiving him about the acquisition of Sardinia,[64] they led him to embrace the ephemeral at the expense of the everlasting. It is difficult to believe that a prince with such sound judgment could ever have trusted them. You can see from this what deceitful means they

---

compensation for the loss of Haute-Navarre. See Roelker, *Queen of Navarre*, 155–85.

60. A reference to the humiliations inflicted upon her by Antoine under the pressure of the Spaniards in the years 1561–1562. Antoine first tried to bring her back into his camp by forcing her to go to Mass, then he disassociated himself from her, drove her from the court, and removed their son from her household to his own. See Roelker, *Queen of Navarre*, 179.

61. In spite of the political and religious instability that characterized the second half of the sixteenth century, Jeanne remained firm in her new faith and devoted her life to fostering Protestantism in Béarn. During the civil wars, she acted as a leader and diplomat of the Huguenot cause. She maintained a lifelong relationship with her mentor Théodore de Bèze, Calvin's lieutenant and successor. See Bernard Roussel, "Jeanne d'Albret et 'ses' théologiens," in *Jeanne d'Albret et sa cour*, 17–18.

62. From an early age, Henri was raised by his mother in the Huguenot faith. His tutors, Pierre Victor Palma-Cayet and François de La Gaucherie, reinforced this leaning, but in March 1562, Jeanne d'Albret was sent away and Henri was forced to remain five years at the Valois court where he would be raised with the royal children. Antoine de Bourbon succumbed to the pressure of Philip II, king of Spain, who first promised him Spanish Navarre, then other lands, if he would raise his son in the Catholic faith and thus promote the Catholic cause. Antoine gave Henri a new Catholic tutor, Jean de Losses, and on June 1, 1562 at Mass in Vincennes, the young boy, aged eight, received the title "Chevalier de l'Ordre," by which he swore to remain Catholic. On this episode, see Albret, *Mémoires et poésies*, 4n1, and Roelker, *Queen of Navarre*, 184. It is interesting to note Jeanne's failure to mention this episode.

63. In 1512, Ferdinand II of Aragon or Ferdinand the Catholic (1452–1516) conquered all Navarre south of the Pyrenées. Antoine de Bourbon's goal to regain the portion of his father-in-law's dominions that Ferdinand had acquired by conquest became "the primary passion of his life, the only fixed star in his firmament and the sole criterion of his political conduct, to which the claims of religion, the preservation of the monarchy and the tranquility of France were all subordinated": Nicola M. Sutherland, *Princes, Politics and Religion, 1547–1589* (London: Hambledon Press, 1984), 56.

64. Both Philip II of Spain and Catherine de' Medici exploited Antoine de Bourbon's obsession with regaining Haute-Navarre. The Catholic-Spanish faction hinted that Antoine might receive the kingdom of Sardinia or the kingdom of Tunis in compensation for the lost territory of Navarre if he would embrace Catholicism. See Roelker, *Queen of Navarre*, 177.

use when they want to lure a person to his ruin. O how many crocodile tears this cardinal[65] shed, and how many cunning ruses[66] he and his brother[67] employed! To really understand these men, it suffices to read the fourth and fifth verses of Psalm 10, that is to say: "His mouth is full of cursing and deceit and fraud: under his tongue is mischief and iniquity."[68] Anyone who has observed the cardinal's facial expressions has seen him feign so naturally kindness, misery and lassitude. The Royal Prophet (David), having encountered similar hypocrites, wanted to [175] mark them so that they would be recognized by all. I must say again how utterly incredible it is that the prince my husband allowed himself to be thus seduced. Like the painter who whitewashes the painted canvas, erasing what was there in order to recreate what pleases him, the Guises erased from my husband's memory the cowardly and mean tricks they had played on him[69] in order to fill his head with new designs.

65. Charles de Lorraine (1524–1574), Archbishop of Reims, and Cardinal de Lorraine, was a political advisor to Henri II and led the French delegation to the Council of Trent. He and his brother, François de Lorraine, were recognized by many as the champions of Catholicism in France. Jeanne depicts him as her primary enemy.

66. These calumnious images of the Reformed rhetoric were advocated by Calvin. See Higman, *The Style of John Calvin*, 123–52.

67. François de Lorraine (1519–1563), second duc de Guise at his father's death in 1550, named lieutenant général de France in 1557 and seen as a military hero. He played a major part in the 1562 Vassy massacre, which set off the French Wars of Religion (1562–1598). His assassination in 1563 by Jean Poltrot de Méré made him a Catholic martyr for France and for the city of Paris.

68. Psalms 10:7 in the Geneva Bible. All future biblical citations refer to this important English-language bible, first published in 1560 and translated by English exiles in Geneva during the reign of Mary I of England. Although Jeanne's references were French-language bibles, the contemporary use, organization and guiding Calvinist doctrine make this a useful translation to use for her biblical citations. Cited here is the 1599 edition with more modernized spelling: *Geneva Bible 1560/1599*, available at GenevaBible.org: <http://www.genevabible.org/Geneva.html>. See also the digitized version of the Geneva 1560 edition at Archive.org: <https://archive.org/details/TheGenevaBible1560>. Judging from the language Jeanne uses, it is obvious that she was working from Clément Marot's poetic adaptation of Psalm 10. Marot (1496–1544) began translating the Psalms into metrical verse most likely at the request of Marguerite de Navarre. Marot was her *valet de chambre* and her protégé. The 1562 Davidic Psalter in the verse translation of Marot and Bèze was very popular at court and the singing of psalms became at that time an important aspect of the Reformed church in France. See Clément Marot and Théodore de Bèze, *Les Psaumes en vers français avec leurs mélodies*. Facsimile reprint of Geneva: Michael Blanchier, 1562, ed. Pierre Pidoux (Geneva: Droz, 1986). On the French Psalter and Reformation propaganda, see Eugénie Droz, "Antoine Vincent : La propagande protestante par le Psaultier," in *Aspects de la propagande religieuse*, ed. Gabrielle Berthoud et al., 276–93 (Geneva: Droz, 1957).

69. Antoine and his brother Louis, prince de Condé, clashed with the house of Guise-Lorraine for influence at court. But what began as political rivalry eventually combined with the conflict that opposed the Catholic Church and the newly Reformed churches.

Among an infinite number of examples of suffering, humiliation, and dishonor that they inflicted on him, I will recount one here, which, if it were fiction
would need a poet to depict it well, and if it were of little consequence, would need
an orator to color it. But the naked truth of this tragicomedy provides its own
ornament. It was during the time that Monsieur the Prince my brother-in-law
was a prisoner in Orléans.[70] Everyone knows that the Guises and their followers
were pursuing the death of the late king my husband[71] in a number of ways: first
by poison, at a dinner which he was warned not to attend, and another evening
when they tried to assassinate him by pistol shot while he was taking leave of
the king. But that time, Monsieur the Constable[72] with his children and other
friends and serviteurs of the lord king my husband escorted him so vigilantly as
he retired to his lodgings that no one could approach him. One might make much
ado of these two attempts if the third by its depravity did not far outdo them.
Having failed [176] at their first two attempts, they persuaded King François, who
is recently deceased,[73] to kill the lord king my husband, in the manner which I
will now describe to you. King François would feign illness. Wearing a simple
shirt and a dagger in his belt, he would send for my husband, who was to come to
his chamber. There he would find only the Sieur de Guise, the Cardinal de Lorraine, the Maréchal de Saint-André,[74] and a few others who had been instructed

70. Louis de Bourbon (1530–1569). See Introduction, note 11.

71. With the accidental death of Henri II on July 10, 1559, the ambitious Guises saw an opportunity
to turn the course of events to their advantage. Under the weak rule of François II who had married
their niece Mary Stuart, their prestige and power as advisors to the king increased. However, Antoine
de Bourbon was first prince of the blood, that is, the next in line for the throne after Henri II's sons, if
they had no male heirs. This rank, in addition to the kingdom of Navarre over which he ruled with his
wife, should have rendered him preeminent in France. However, on March 25, 1561, Antoine agreed to
renounce his claim to the regency in exchange for the title of lieutenant général of the kingdom, which
gave him military authority superior to that of the Constable, Guise, and all the marshals of France
combined. On the attitude of François II and the Guises toward Antoine de Bourbon in May–June
1560, see Roelker, *Queen of Navarre,* 135–38.

72. Anne de Montmorency (1493–1567), military leader, statesman, diplomat, named grand maître de
France in 1526 and connétable de France in 1538. He was an intimate of François I, and the confidant
and chief advisor of Henri II, but his political influence waned when the power of the Guise brothers
increased during the brief reign of François II (1559–1560). Montmorency had to give up his grand
maître status to the duc de Guise. However, when Catherine de' Medici, under the influence of chancellor Michel de L'Hôpital, began to advocate a policy of compromise and concessions in favor of the
Protestants, Montmorency joined forces with his former enemy, François de Guise, and with him and
Jacques d'Albon formed the Triumvirate, an association in defense of Catholicism.

73. François II died at the age of 16 on December 5, 1560, after less than two years as king. In 1558
he had married Mary Stuart, queen of Scots (1543–1567), and was greatly influenced by her uncles,
the Guises.

74. Jacques d'Albon (c.1505–1562), named by Henri II maréchal de France under the name of
Saint-André. He died at the battle of Dreux on December 19, 1562.

about what to do. The king would start a quarrel with my husband over something trivial, "une querelle d'Allemaigne," as they say; then the king would stab him with his dagger, and the others would finish him off. This was decided, after a debate among several of those present. There were differing opinions; some could not consent to such cruelty, which would sully the hand of our young king with his own blood. Nevertheless, the Guises' ambition and desire to reign prompted them to choose a course of action which is not only criminal, but utterly barbaric and more expected of Cannibals, who eat one another and do not know God, than of those who have learned of him but do not believe.[75]

After this had been decided, the queen was informed by the king himself, or by someone else, and she did the late king my husband the favor and the honor to have him warned[76] by Madame la duchesse de Montpensier.[77] Indeed, I recall that her majesty often said to me that the late king my husband owed his life to her, and that if [177] the duchesse de Montpensier were still alive, she would bear witness to that debt. Following this ungodly counsel, and in spite of some opposition, the late King François sent for my husband to come alone and speak with him in his chamber (where King François, too, was alone, except for those who were part of the conspiracy). The king my husband was advised not to go there, and to find some excuse, which he did. King François sent for him a second time, and he was again warned not to go by someone who told him the truth about their intentions. In the end, urged by his magnanimous heart and the pure conscience that prevented him from fearing this death, he resolved to go with only a few of his men, including Capitaine Ranty,[78] a lieutenant in his company whom he trusted and who had been raised with him. As he climbed the stairs to the king's chamber, he met someone who tried to stop him by saying: "Sire, why are you going to your ruin?" However, determined as he was, he turned back toward the captain and said, "Capitaine Ranty, I am about to enter a place where they have plotted my death, but never did a skin cost so dearly as mine will cost them. God willing, I will be saved, but I ask you, by the loyalty I have always known in you, the noble upbringing we shared, and the friendship I have shown you, to do me this last service: if I should die, [178]

75. Compare Jeanne's observation to Montaigne's in "On the Cannibals" (*Essay* I, 31): "So we can indeed call those folk barbarians by the rules of reason but not in comparison with ourselves, who surpass them in every kind of barbarism." Michel de Montaigne, *The Complete Essays*, ed. and trans. M. A. Screech (London: Allen Lane, 1991), 236.

76. A plot to assassinate Antoine de Bourbon and thus eliminate a high-ranking noble capable of challenging the Guises' power would certainly not have been in Catherine's interest at a time when she was attempting to play the nobles against each other to protect her son's authority.

77. Jacqueline de Longwy (c. 1520–August 28, 1561), duchesse de Montpensier, wife of Louis de Bourbon-Montpensier, prince of the blood; intimate of Catherine de' Medici. According to Roelker, she and her two sisters "never officially left the Roman Church, but they openly advocated reform and protected persons accused of outright heresy": "The Appeal of Calvinism," 399.

78. Capitaine Jacques de Ranty, lieutenant of Antoine de Bourbon's personal guard.

you will retrieve the shirt I am now wearing, and take it, bloodied, to my wife and to my son. And beseech my wife, in the name of the great love that she has always borne me, and in the name of duty (for my son is not yet old enough to avenge my death), to send my torn and bloody shirt, for if I die she will,[79] to foreign princes and Christians so that they will avenge such a cruel and treacherous murder." And upon those words he entered the king's chamber, where the Cardinal de Lorraine immediately shut the door behind him from the inside. The king had some harsh words for him, to which he responded with duty and reverence, while keeping an eye on his enemies. This surprised them, and the confrontation played out in words. The duc de Guise and his brother, having retreated to a window, referred to the king in a manner befitting their impudence: "Here is the most cowardly heart there ever was." Thereupon, opening the door, they left.

There is no doubt that the Almighty God, who reigns in the fury of the wicked and holds in the palm of his hand the hearts of kings, here touched one and the other. He kept our sovereign king from committing parricide, such a cowardly act against his own blood, and by preventing this, he stoked the flames of fury burning these traitors. God made clear to the king my husband that he is an attentive father to us, his children, and [179] will not allow a single hair to fall from our heads unless he wills it,[80] no matter how confident the wicked are in their plots.

This is what I understood of the situation based on what I heard from the late king my husband and Capitaine Ranty. I wanted to refresh my memory later but was unable to learn more from the king my husband, as the Guises had already begun to dominate him. And because I opposed the Guises's damnable ways and because they feared I would thwart their plan by filling his ears with these incidents from the past, they had me sent away.[81] The king my husband clearly held them responsible for this. When the cardinal, who had promised him not to pursue the marriage of his brother the grand prior[82] with Madame de Nevers[83] (who is now Madame de Longueville) and had nonetheless underhandedly sent a messenger, my husband became so angry that he rejected the cardinal's

---

79. Translating the word *fera* as it appears in the 1570 edition; but if this is a printing error for *sera*, the meaning would be: "to send my torn and bloody shirt, as it *will be* if I die."

80. Matthew 10:30; Luke 12:7.

81. In March 1562, under pressure of both the Guises and Philip II of Spain, having failed to convert Jeanne back to Catholicism, Antoine de Bourbon expelled her from the court. Clearly, Jeanne held the Guises responsible for her expulsion. See Roelker, *Queen of Navarre*, 179–81.

82. François de Lorraine (1534–1563), younger brother of François de Guise and Charles de Lorraine.

83. Marie de Bourbon (1539–1601), duchesse d'Estouteville, was first married to Jean de Bourbon, seigneur d'Enghien, a brother of Antoine de Bourbon. After his death, she married François I de Clèves, duc de Nevers, a cousin and former brother-in-law of Antoine de Bourbon. After François's death in 1562, Marie married Léonor d'Orléans, duc de Longueville.

excuses and invoked all that he had done for him. He reproached him: "You made me send my wife away, break with my brother (speaking of Monsieur le Prince de Condé), and dismiss my best serviteurs, and then you come here to trick me." If only he had remained as lucid as he was at that moment, he would perhaps still be alive. And, given his deathbed testimony,[84] I am certain that if he were alive today [180] he would be where his son is now.[85] But Madame de Guise[86] came to see him that night and reconciled him with the Guises.

This is how, abusing his goodness, they made him play such a shameful role at the end of his life at the expense of his reputation. I wonder therefore how the queen who is well aware of their disgraceful behavior, can allow a man as violent as the cardinal near our king, and how she does not fear that he will do her or the king some bad turn. Indeed, how can one trust bloodthirsty people whose cruel nature cannot be kept in check by anything, be it the fear of God, honor, honesty, blood ties, shame, any friendship or obligation? This is what I said in the letter I wrote to her majesty after I heard directly from her what displeasure she felt at the sight of the late king my husband being misled this way. Hoping that one day she will read this, I beg her very humbly to remember the regret she shared with me about this at Saint Germain[87] and how troubled she was that the Maréchal de Saint-André and the Cardinal de Tournon[88] led my husband to Paris to speak to the court of the parlement and to prevent the publication of the January Edict.[89] Although she, too, went to Paris later, it was to no avail.[90]

84. According to his Huguenot physician and friend, Raphael de Taillevis, Antoine returned to some form of Protestantism in the last hours of his life. Bordenave questions the sincerity of this supposed conversion. Bordenave, *Histoire de Béarn et Navarre*, 114.

85. Henri was fighting for the Protestant cause during the Third War of Religion.

86. Anne d'Este (1531–1607), eldest child of Renée de France and Ercole d'Este, duke of Ferrara, in 1548 married François de Lorraine, who became second duc de Guise in 1550.

87. Jeanne and the queen may have felt on the same side at the time, since Antoine, had he remained Protestant, could have counterbalanced the Guises' unchecked power, which was against Jeanne's and Catherine's political interests.

88. François de Tournon (1489–1562), made cardinal in 1530, a skilled diplomat who filled the function of foreign minister and was entrusted with several delicate negotiations under the reign of François I and Henri II. He spent the last part of his life fighting against the Huguenots. It was the Cardinal de Tournon who had performed the marriage of Jeanne d'Albret to the duc de Clèves on June 14, 1541.

89. The Edict of January was signed by the twelve-year-old king Charles IX on January 17, 1562, at Saint-Germain-en-Laye. Calvinists were permitted to worship in the outskirts of towns and in the countryside under the supervision of the civil authorities. They could use their churches as before, but could not build new ones. The parlement of Paris, defying the young king and his mother, initially refused to register the Edict.

90. Albret, *Mémoires et poésies*, 16n5 cites Claude Haton's *Mémoires*, which reports that Catherine de' Medici rode by herself to Paris on February 19, 1562, to persuade the parlement to register the

She knows how much she relied on me at Saint Germain during the time that this Edict was being debated,[91] whether that meant speaking to the late king my husband to try to mollify him or reporting to her what I was able to learn, [181] her majesty being at that time sympathetic to the cause of the Reform.[92] If it pleases her, this will remind her of the peepholes she had made, from her chamber into that of the late king my husband, at Saint Germain en Laye, in order to eavesdrop on the councils held by the Cardinal de Tournon, the Maréchal de Saint-André, d'Escars,[93] and others, and from my own chamber into that of the Cardinal de Tournon. Did she not find me loyal in all this?[94] Because it concerned first, the glory of God, and second, the good of the kingdom, I opened my eyes to the duty of my soul while shutting them to the affection for a husband. I even showed her letters that Versigny, the Prevost des marchands,[95] had brought to the late king my husband, signed by the Lords of Guise and others who were in Paris where Versigny was going to meet up with them later.

It is not without reason that I also remind the queen of Fontainebleau. When I left her one evening, she was determined to depart for Orléans.[96] But I knew that she was vacillating in this decision, so the next morning I went to find her in a garden where she was having a milking shed built. There I pointed out the harm she would do to herself if she did not continue the voyage and how she would thus prevent those whom she had made take up arms from serving her and the king as they wished to do.[97] After we debated many things from one side and the other, she assured me that she would leave in eight days. However, later [182]

Edict of January: *Mémoires de Claude Haton contenant le récit des événements accomplis de 1553 à 1582, principalement dans la Champagne et la Brie*, publiés par Félix Bourquelot, 2 vols (Paris: Imprimerie impériale, 1857), 1:187.

91. A reference to the strong opposition against the Edict's registration after it was promulgated by the king on January 17, 1562. The members of the parlement of Paris, among others, immediately attacked it, but were forced to register it on March 6, 1562.

92. In 1562, Catherine de' Medici had not given up on her moderate position, hoping for a compromise between Catholic and Protestant nobles and a balance of influences at court.

93. François Peyrusse, comte des Cars or d'Escars (d. 1595), a Catholic, and an intimate of the Guises; appointed lieutenant général in Guyenne in 1561, and governor of Bordeaux in 1565. In 1579 he married Blaise de Monluc's widow, Isabeau de Beauville.

94. On Jeanne's self-representation as dutiful subject, see Pascal, *Lettres de la Royne de Navarre*, 246–47.

95. Guillaume de Marle, sieur de Versigny. According to Albret, *Mémoires et poésies*, 18n2, these letters may have been the protestation of the assembly of the notables of Paris against the Edict of January.

96. Condé, the major leader of the French Protestants was soon to set up headquarters in the city of Orléans.

97. Catherine de' Medici had addressed four letters to Condé, recommending to him the interests of the king: *Lettres de Catherine de Médicis*, ed. Hector de la Ferrière et al. (Paris: Imprimerie nationale, 1880), 1: 281–84, and Albret, *Mémoires et poésies*, 19n2.

at dinner, she concluded with the king's maîtres d'hôtel[98] and lords to spend Lent at Fontainebleau, persuaded by those around her of the devotion of the Guises, and still believing that she could escape whenever she wanted, which, when the time came, she was unable to do.[99]

During that time, as I was sick in bed,[100] her majesty, considering on the one hand that something was being plotted in Paris against her will, and on the other what she and Monsieur le Prince my brother[101] had determined through letters, messages, and the intermediary of the Sieur de Bouchavannes,[102] sent me a maître des requêtes[103] of the king named Belesbat.[104] Through him she instructed me with much firmness (even though I considered the least of her commands an honor and a favor) to send one of my men secretly to the Prince de Condé, my brother-in-law, and to Monsieur l'Amiral[105] to warn them not to believe anything signed by the king, nor sealed with his seal, for from that time on he would be doing everything under duress. At her command, I sent one of my men, Brandon,[106] also known as Bladre, who is now maître d'hôtel of Monsieur de Longueville.[107] I deem her a princess so virtuous and honest that she will always acknowledge that particular service,[108] as will the person who told me so on her behalf (which she later confirmed to me personally),

98. The important post of maître d'hôtel was given to a nobleman in the royal household who was to oversee the management of the kitchen and servants.

99. The queen mother was avoiding Paris for fear that she and her son would be taken hostage by the triumvirs, an outcome that would nonetheless transpire. On March 27, 1562, in order to lend legitimacy to their cause, the triumvirs accompanied by Antoine de Bourbon forcibly escorted the king and his mother from Fontainebleau to Paris.

100. From an early age, Jeanne was in poor health. Like her mother, she would regularly visit the baths in Béarn for their therapeutic effect. According to historians, her poor state of health was often a concern for those around her; see, for example, *Lettres d'Antoine de Bourbon et de Jehanne d'Albret*, ed. Mis de Rochambeau (Paris: Renouard, 1877), 75–76 and 128–29. At age 44, she succumbed to yet another bout of what was likely tuberculosis.

101. Jeanne frequently calls her brother-in-law, the Prince of Condé, "mon frere."

102. Antoine de Bayancourt, sieur de Bouchavannes, Condé's companion in arms.

103. A high-ranking magistrate.

104. Perhaps Robert Hurault, seigneur de Belesbat, maître des requêtes of the king in 1562, and son-in-law of Michel de L'Hôpital. See Arlette Jouanna et al., *Histoire et dictionnaire des guerres de religion* (Paris: R. Laffont, 1998), 985.

105. That is to say, Coligny. See Introduction, note 12.

106. Victor Brodeau, sieur de la Chassetière, secretary of the king and queen of Navarre, entrusted with many delicate missions. He would be part of Jeanne's council in La Rochelle and would later serve as a diplomat in the service of her son.

107. Léonor d'Orléans, duc de Longueville.

108. In early 1562, Jeanne's relationship to the queen was friendly enough for Jeanne to appeal to the memory of these days. At times, their respective predicaments brought them into close cooperation.

Brandon the messenger, and the others who received the message and [183] the letter of credence[109] from me. Upon his return from Paris, my husband the king made me immediately leave court, so that the members of the court and I left Fontainebleau at the same time.[110]

I will not expand on the voyage of the court, since others have written about it, and instead will recount my own. I will not forget the honor and favor that I received at my departure from the king, the queen, and Monsieur[111] when they commanded me to identify one of my serviteurs through whom we could communicate, either with letters of credence, or should I trust him, without a letter, about how best to serve them. I did so, and named Brandon, who had already served in this capacity. I am certain that my son has a good enough memory to recall this. My son designated the Sieur de Beauvoir,[112] at that time maître de chambre[113] and now his preceptor, who could be trusted to tell me whatever they wanted me to know. Their majesties assured me of the confidence they placed in those who had taken up arms at their order[114] and directed me to see them when I traveled through Orléans, and tell them a number of things on their behalf. The late king my husband expressly forbade this (I still have the letter in this regard[115]) and thus prevented me from doing so. But while I was in the village of Olivet,[116] the seigneurs who were in Orléans[117] sent me Monsieur de Bèze, to whom I told everything.

After I arrived at my home in Vendôme, I sent Brandon back to the [184] queen, and when he returned he brought me some letters in which she

---

On the relations between Jeanne d'Albret et Catherine de' Medici see Roelker, *Queen of Navarre*, 326–53.

109. Regarding letters of credence, see Introduction, 19.

110. Jeanne and the court did not leave at exactly the same time. The court left Fontainebleau on March 31, 1562, while Jeanne was already on her way to Meaux on March 27, when the triumvirs arrived in Fontainebleau.

111. Henri, brother of Charles IX and future Henri III of France.

112. Louis de Goulard, sieur de Beauvoir, tutor of Henri de Béarn in his early childhood; reinstated as Henri's tutor after the death of Antoine de Bourbon. A member of Jeanne's entourage, he became her friend and counselor in later years. See Roelker, *Queen of Navarre*, 189.

113. This was a prestigious position in a noble household given to a nobleman close to the lord (or lady) and often involving personal and delicate diplomatic tasks.

114. See Catherine de' Medici's letter to Condé expressing the confidence she places in him and asking him to protect her and her children: *Lettres de Catherine de Médicis*, 1: 283.

115. This letter could not be found.

116. A village five kilometers south of Orléans.

117. Condé and Coligny had taken Orléans on April 2, 1562.

commanded me to ask Monsieur le Prince my brother-in-law to lay down his arms.[118] However, the opinion of the messenger was that des Cars, having entered her chamber in order to make her write that letter, had not left her side while she was writing. This was the reason why she was forced to write the opposite of the opinion she had expressed to the gentleman. He furthermore told me, on her behalf, that if I saw things going so badly that the king was being even more closely guarded, I was to go to Amboise[119] under the pretense of going to pay my respects to Monsieur le Duc, who was called at that time Monsieur d'Anjou,[120] and to Madame Marguerite, sister of the king,[121] and that I bring them to Orléans. And to that end, the sieur de La Bourdaisière[122] had orders to allow me to enter Amboise, accompanied by whomever I wished.

What prevented me from carrying out those instructions was the authorization the late king my husband gave me to retire to my home in Béarn. I did so, and just in time, for if I had waited eight days to leave, I would have been imprisoned in one of my husband's houses, as he had promised the Cardinal de Lorraine. And when he made that promise, the venerable cardinal went so far as to declare solemnly: "Monsieur, that is an act worthy of you! God grant you a long and good life." But Brandon, whom I had sent to the queen, and who brought me a new [185] order from the late king my husband to stop at Vendôme,[123] found me already at Châtellerault.[124] So I completed my journey and came to Caumont[125] where I had to stop because of illness. I nevertheless tried hard to restore order

118. Catherine de' Medici's letter to Jeanne has been lost, but Jeanne's reply has been reproduced in *Lettres d'Antoine de Bourbon et de Jehanne d'Albret*, 251–52. In this letter she diplomatically declines to take the requested action.

119. A royal residence.

120. Last son of Henri II and Catherine de' Medici, François Hercule d'Anjou (1554–1584), duc d'Alençon, became duc d'Anjou after the Peace of Beaulieu in 1576.

121. On August 18, 1572, Marguerite (1553–1615), princess of France, daughter of Henri II and Catherine de' Medici, and a Catholic, was wedded to Henri III de Navarre, a Protestant, in a failed attempt of reconciliation.

122. Jean Babou, seigneur de La Bourdaisière, cupbearer to the king and queen of Navarre, grand master of the artillery of France in 1567, died October 11, 1569.

123. Vendôme was the seat of Antoine's family, and Jeanne was merely duchess. There were rumors that Antoine intended to imprison her there.

124. Jeanne had been told to confine herself to the duchy of Vendôme, but she does not appear to have done so. Châtellerault is situated at some 30 kilometers northeast of Poitiers.

125. Although there is no written evidence of definite orders from Antoine de Bourbon to capture Jeanne after she left Vendôme, she had reasons to believe that Monluc was to prevent her from escaping into Béarn. On July 22, 1562, she took refuge in the impregnable château of Caumont (Lot-et-Garonne), property of François Nompar de Caumont de la Force, a Huguenot who supported the crown: Roelker, *Queen of Navarre*, 195. He was killed during the Saint Bartholomew's Day Massacre.

there in Guyenne[126] with the late Monsieur de Burie and Monluc,[127] and, though they do not credit me, to convince Monsieur de Duras[128] to return to Orléans. There are still those in Guyenne who know, including Monsieur de Caumont, the zeal I showed for both the glory of God and service to the king. But because the Cardinal de Lorraine schemed at that time with his brother the Sieur de Guise and made him play along, the Sieur de Burie and Monluc were separated, and each out of jealousy toward the other competed to do the worst that he could against those of the Reformed faith. When I saw that I was not able to do what I desired in Guyenne, I sent my maître d'hôtel named Roques[129] to the queen. Through him she informed me that she approved of everything that I had done, complaining emphatically about the late king my husband, and about the limited means she had to do what she had wanted to do. When I realized that I had become ineffectual in this matter, and that I was no longer being utilized, and was warned that Monluc had been given the charge to arrest me, I retired to Nérac, and from there to Béarn. It may seem superfluous to speak about my own affairs [186], nonetheless, to make known to everyone the long-standing malice of the Cardinal de Lorraine and his brother the Sieur de Guise, I will say that the cardinal went to the Council[130] leaving his brother well instructed. He pressured the late king my husband to send one of his secretaries, named Boulogne,[131] to my court of parlement at Pau with orders to abolish all exercise of the Reformed faith that I had introduced in Béarn (with his consent), and to deprive all those who were not Catholic of religious services. My husband did not want anyone of the Reformed faith to remain in the country.[132] He had directed Boulogne not to speak with me

126. When Charles de Coucy, seigneur de Burie and the king's lieutenant général in Guyenne, was unable to restore peace in Guyenne in 1561, Charles IX and Catherine de' Medici sent Blaise de Monluc to assist him. Jeanne's strategy was to separate Monluc from Burie and thus neutralize the influence of both men with the parlement of Bordeaux: see Roelker, *Queen of Navarre*, 194; Bryson, *Queen Jeanne*, 147.

127. Blaise de Montesquiou de Lasseran-Massencôme, seigneur de Monluc (c. 1502–1577), known as Blaise de Monluc. A military leader who served under five kings, François I, Henri II, François II, Charles IX, and Henri III, he was named marshall of France by Henri III in 1574.

128. Symphorien de Durfort, seigneur de Duras, leading Huguenot commander of the Protestant forces in Guyenne. He made an unsuccessful attempt to take Bordeaux. Duras's Protestant army was defeated by Monluc's army at the battle of Vergt (midway between Bergerac and Périgueux) on October 9, 1562. See on this decisive battle Bryson, *Queen Jeanne*, 146–47.

129. Jean de Secondat, seigneur de Roques, maître d'hôtel of the queen of Navarre.

130. The Cardinal de Lorraine was in Rome from 1562 to 1563 to attend late sessions of the Council of Trent, which convened intermittently from 1545 to 1563, with the aim of reestablishing Catholic unity and condemning what were viewed as Protestant heresies.

131. Jean Lescripvain, seigneur de Boulogne, Antoine de Bourbon's secretary.

132. As early as July 1561, public worship and freedom were permitted for the Protestant ministers to use churches for worship at certain times of the day while Roman Catholics continued to use them at

about it at all. When I learned this, I availed myself of the natural power over my subjects which God had given me, but which I had relinquished to a husband[133] out of the obedience that God commands that we show them.[134] But when I saw that the glory of God and the purity of service to him were at stake, I had Boulogne taken prisoner, and I kept his packet of letters.

Soon afterward I lost the Sieur my husband,[135] as attested in my letter to the queen, and I would rather say as little as possible regarding the disfavor shown me and my son as a result of this loss, so I will only select three or four incidents from an infinite number. The first was when I was persuaded, with sweet promises and flattery, to join the court on its voyage to Lyon,[136] having been assured [187] that the many concerns that I had previously expressed regarding Monluc and other matters would be resolved to my satisfaction. However, when I arrived in Roussillon,[137] I was unable to obtain what I requested.

It seems to me that it would not be out of place to mention an incident that happened in Roussillon that will lead any Christian of good judgment to admire the providence of Almighty God. He surprises the clever in their cleverness, and the wise of the world in their wisdom by using means both surprising and feeble to vanquish the strong.[138] In Roussillon, where the court was staying in July 1564, I had been given a very small chamber. One day one of my women took some letters away from my little dog who was playing with them. She gave them to me, thinking that I had lost them. I recognized the handwriting of the queen on a letter and thought that it had fallen out of one of my chests. In order to decide whether it was

---

other times (a policy known as *simultaneum*). However, full implementation of Jeanne's religious policies was delayed by the difficulties created by Antoine, who repeatedly tried to convince the Catholic leaders of his cooperation. See Roelker, *Queen of Navarre*, 198.

133. For the first time in the *Declaration*, Jeanne refers to Antoine as *a* husband ("*un* mary"), transferring her loyalty and the possessive adjective from husband to God ("mon Dieu").

134. Reminiscent of a passage from St. Paul, Ephesians 5:22–25.

135. Antoine de Bourbon was wounded during the Catholic siege of Rouen on October 16, 1562. He died of his wound on November 17, and was buried in the Bourbon family chapel of the Church of Saint Georges in Vendôme.

136. This was the grand tour of the realm of France that Catherine de' Medici had set up on January 24, 1564, to show the fourteen-year-old Charles IX his war-torn kingdom and introduce him to his deeply divided subjects. See Victor. E. Graham and W. McAllister Johnson, *The Royal Tour of France by Charles IX and Catherine de' Medici: Festivals and Entries, 1564–1566* (Toronto: Toronto University Press, 1979).

137. A village just south of Lyon, where the queen mother stopped before the royal grand tour of France in July 1564. Jeanne's purpose in meeting the queen there seems to have been "to accuse Monluc of treason, and so have him removed from the lieutenant-generalship of Guyenne": Bryson, *Queen Jeanne*, 162. Monluc remained in his position but the Protestant Antoine d'Aure, seigneur de Gramont was named lieutenant général for Béarn.

138. Cf. 1 Corinthians 1:27–29.

important enough either to lock it up or to destroy it, I read the first word which said "Monsieur," and reading what was written above, I saw that it was addressed to the king of Spain.[139] I was very surprised, for I feared that someone had planted it in my chamber in order to turn her majesty against me. Also, I considered that only a few of my people and a handful of my friends had come into my chamber. After eating in [188] another room, I had retired to my chamber because of the excessive heat with only two or three of my women. I could not figure out where the letter had come from; all I knew was that my little dog was playing with it in my chamber. I read it, and because it had been written during the time of the first troubles, we were disparaged in a curious fashion. In this letter, her majesty beseeched the king of Spain to help her against the subversives and the rebels who wanted to remove the crown from the head of the king her son, and that her only hope for justice was through him. Reading this caused me great distress, because these words seemed to me so inopportune that her majesty would be troubled that this letter had been discovered. On the other hand, I feared that because I was unable to provide her a better explanation of where it came from, she would think that I had obtained it by some unscrupulous means. Finally, I resolved to deliver it to her, convinced that she would do me the honor of believing me honest, and I took the letter to her chamber. The queen sent for the Sieur de L'Aubespine, the *secrétaire d'état*[140] charged with dispatches from Spain, and had him read the letter in the presence of Madame de Savoie[141] who was there with her. Indeed she honored those of the faith by courteously apologizing for the words used in the letter. She assured me that she had never believed us to be subversives or rebels, but she had been forced to write that way, and in that time of war many things had been [189] said and written that should no longer be recalled. The Sieur de L'Aubespine assured her that the letter had been delivered to Spain, and that she had received a response. Whereupon they speculated about where it had come from: some said that some Huguenots had had it stolen, others said that it was Catholics who had done so, and still others said that some foreign ambassador had procured it in order to incite us against one another. However, none of them was on the mark as I discovered only the next day (I had not had the time to make any more enquiries before that because I delivered the letter to the queen the very hour I found it). Once back in my chamber, I was told that someone had seen my dog pick up the

139. Philip II (1527–1598). See Introduction, note 22.

140. Claude de L'Aubespine (1510–1567), *secrétaire d'état* and close advisor of Catherine de' Medici, who was commissioned on several occasions to negotiate with the Protestants in the king's name: Jouanna et al., *Histoire et dictionnaire*, 166. The position of *secrétaire d'état* was still evolving at the end of the sixteenth century. He would be one of several men responsible for royal correspondence involving financial engagements both within France and with foreign countries.

141. Marguerite de France (1523–1574), daughter of François I and Claude de France, sister of Henri II and sister-in-law of Catherine de' Medici. She became duchesse de Savoie by her marriage to duc Emmanuel-Philibert de Savoie.

letter from a pile of sweepings in front of Madame de Guise's chamber which was next to mine, as the dog often did with papers and other debris. Our chambers exited into a long gallery from which my little dog had brought the letter. I told this to the queen, who, for a number of reasons, did not doubt that the letter had come from there, and that it could have been sent to the Cardinal de Lorraine. All this is to show how God reveals things that we believe are kept most secret,[142] as he did with this letter, by which the queen can recognize what covert information Spain had about those of the faith and the cunning way [190] and the "seemly" terms in which these gentlemen forced her majesty to write about us.

I retired from Roussillon, as I was ill,[143] and during my absence the voyage was made to Bayonne,[144] where were forged the blades of the swords that today are spilling Christian blood.[145] To turn to other incidents demonstrating my fall from favor (since I digressed in explaining the first so as not to overlook what happened in Roussillon), I will now address the injustice that was done to me after the wedding of Monsieur le Prince my brother-in-law,[146] after I came back to court,[147] through Moulins,[148] and on to Paris.[149] In a time of peace, my county of Foix and my cities of Pamiers and Foix[150] were pillaged and ravaged by garrisons

142. This idea that God sees and knows everything is a leitmotif in the Psalms; see 7:10; 44:21; 94:11, among others.

143. It was in Crémieu (Isère), on July 9, that Jeanne, for reasons of health, requested to return to her domains. She was instructed by the queen to take up residence in Vendôme where she would be farther from the Spanish frontier. Jeanne's presence at the Bayonne interview, where Catherine de' Medici was about to meet the Catholic champions from Spain, was judged inopportune. See Roelker, *Queen of Navarre*, 231.

144. Catherine de' Medici's pretext for this stop in Bayonne (in Jeanne's territories) was to see her daughter Elisabeth, queen of Spain, but the true object of her journey was to meet with Elisabeth's husband, King Philip II of Spain. Philip, who found Catherine de' Medici's policy of compromise unacceptable, sent in his place his minister and counsellor, Fernando Alvarez de Toledo, Duke of Alva, reputed to be inflexible.

145. There were rumors that the duke of Alva had argued in response to the Protestant insurrection in the neighboring Low Countries for the banishment of Calvinist ministers from France and the annihilation of heretics. See Sutherland, *Princes, Politics and Religion*, 163–64.

146. After the death of Éléonore de Roye, Louis de Bourbon married Françoise d'Orléans-Longueville.

147. Jeanne met the court in Moulins in January 1566. See Albret, *Mémoires et poésies*, 38n2.

148. The court stayed three months in Moulins, from December 22, 1565 to March 23, 1566. See Albret, *Mémoires et poésies*, 38n3.

149. The court arrived in Paris on May 1, 1566. See Albret, *Mémoires et poésies*, 38n4.

150. The situation in Foix and Pamiers exemplified Jeanne's ambiguous position as both a sovereign queen and a subject of the French crown. Foix was the ancestral home of the Albret family but lay in French territory. When the Bishop sought help from the French crown in eliminating Protestant services, he prevailed over Jeanne's defense of the rights of Protestants there. When the Protestants in Foix and Pamiers resisted in 1566, the parlement of Toulouse sent in military forces. Jeanne saw this

and commissions, for which I was denied justice and deprived of the privileges accorded by kings to my ancestors.

Furthermore, who was not scandalized by the deliberate injustice that was done to me at that time in the person of my cousin of Rohan.[151] In the decree pronounced against her in his private council, the king abided by the opinion of seven members, among whom there were only two jurisconsults.[152] This was in opposition to the opinion of eighteen or nineteen voters, chosen from both the grand and the private councils, judged to be the most sincere and knowledgeable, but whose honesty and knowledge, I contend, served only as a cover. The decree bears these words: "for this case only, without setting precedent," because [191] the referral of her case to the pope was directly against the privileges of the Gallican Church. Nevertheless, to make the injustice ever more unjust, the following day the Cardinal de Lorraine allowed them to become engaged[153] and then married them,[154] in contradiction with the decree pronounced by his own authority, and in disregard of their Holy Father. Hence the cardinal was not so very Roman Catholic, since he preferred his ambition to his religion when he pressed ahead with the nuptials, despite a properly filed objection on the part of my cousin of Rohan.[155] If I described this injurious injustice more fully than the others, it is

---

as lack of respect for her as a queen whereas the crown deemed the Protestants in this area to be in violation of the terms of the Edict of Amboise. See Roelker, *Queen of Navarre*, 239.

151. A notorious scandal of sixteenth-century France, which divided the country between the partisans of the House of Guise and the partisans of the House of Bourbon. In 1557, Françoise de Rohan (1548–1590), first cousin to Jeanne and a lady-in-waiting to Catherine de' Medici, instituted a suit against Jacques de Savoie, duc de Nemours, to recognize formally their orally-agreed marriage contract and the child that she had with him. The case was reopened after the assassination of the duc de Guise, in 1563, when Anne d'Este, his widow, and Jacques de Savoie married. On April 28, 1566, the King's council confirmed the judgment of the Primate of Gaul (Archbishop of Lyon) against Françoise. Jeanne openly defended Françoise and challenged the competence of the members of the King's council. The child from this unofficial union was raised in Jeanne's household. She stubbornly continued to call him "mon neveu Nemours." On the Rohan case, see the two letters Antoine de Bourbon addressed to Jeanne in 1560 in *Lettres d'Antoine de Bourbon et de Jehanne d'Albret*, 222–25. See also Roelker, *Queen of Navarre*, 244–46; Matthew A. Vester, *Jacques de Savoie-Nemours: L'apanage du Genevois au cœur de la puissance dynastique savoyarde au XVIe siècle*, trans. Éléonore Mazel (Geneva: Droz, 2008), 67–98; and Una McIlvenna, "Word Versus Honor: The Case of Françoise de Rohan vs. Jacques de Savoie," *Journal of Early Modern History* 16, no. 4–5 (2012): 315–34.

152. Christophe de Thou and Pierre Séguier. See Albret, *Mémoires et poésies*, 39n3.

153. This happened on April 29, 1566, the day after judgment was rendered against Françoise de Rohan.

154. The marriage was celebrated on May 5, 1566, in the presence of the king and the court. See McIlvenna, "Word Versus Honor," 330.

155. This opposition was delivered on behalf of Françoise de Rohan by a judicial officer, Vincent Petit, who was immediately arrested and imprisoned. See Albret, *Mémoires et poésies*, 42n1.

because not everyone who reads this will know the truth of the situation, and because this is the injustice that caused me the most grief.

I could attest to numerous vexations, especially if I were to point out that some fools dared fill the ears of the queen with an absurd lie. The impudence of such a lie bore its own proof. They wanted her to believe that I had instigated two plots. First, to put it bluntly, I supposedly wanted to have her throat cut. Secondly, they claimed that I wanted to have Monsieur the brother of the king kidnapped in order to strengthen my position and create dissension in France against the king. No matter how humbly and earnestly I entreated her majesty, I could never find out from her who denounced me, except for ambiguous hints. [192] She wanted me to be satisfied with her assurance that she did not believe any of it. She attempted to make me suspicious of four or five people, and, in the end, I pressed her so much that upon our arrival at Monceaux,[156] she enlightened me a bit more. While these things were happening, over a period of four or five months, did the poor Savigny,[157] believed to be a bastard son of the late king my husband, not die an innocent man? The Guises, authors of the lie that they shrewdly had circulated by a third party, and driven by their hatred for Savigny, said to the queen that he wanted to assassinate her. For a while now, that accusation has carried such weight that, even without legitimacy or plausibility, those suspected or named by the Guises were killed no matter what the price, like Savigny himself. They killed under the queen's name, a thing so loathsome and deplorable that it is unthinkable to me that she could have consented to it or even known about it. The Spaniard who killed Savigny in the fields with a pistol had previously served him, then left him for a time, and later returned to his service. After the deed was done, he was arrested and taken to Fort l'Évêque.[158] While he was there, he asked several times for an Italian who was staying with the sieur de l'Aubespine.[159] The Italian [193] knew well that the Spaniard had killed Savigny under orders, and who had made him do it. The other prisoners, too, reported this to someone worthy of confidence, and one night the Spaniard, after having told his story, was removed from prison and thrown into the river with a rock tied around his neck. That is how these evil souls want to shake up heaven and earth, and by their malice overthrow piety and justice, and poison the mind of our young, naturally good king with their venom-

---

156. Located a few miles from Meaux, Montceaux-lés-Meaux (Seine-et-Marne) is known for its sumptuous château which was given, in 1556, to Catherine de' Medici by Henri II and, later, to Gabrielle d'Estrées by Henri IV. Very little is left of it today. See Théophile Lhuillier, "L'ancien château royal de Montceaux en Brie," in *Bureau des musées ... et de l'inventaire des richesses d'art de la France* (N.p.: n.p., 1884), 246–83.

157. No information could be found about this character or the events reported here.

158. The prison of Four-l'Évêque or Fort-l'Évêque was located on the rue de l'Arbre Sec in the Quartier Saint-Germain in Paris. See Albret, *Mémoires et poésies*, 44n1.

159. See above, note 140.

ous temperament. I could speak of my legitimate complaints, which motivated me to write many letters without ever obtaining satisfaction. But I would digress from my intention to speak only of three occasions that led me to join with the Princes, gentlemen, and other faithful serviteurs of God and of the king for the just cause, from which (as I demonstrated above) I never deviated, and even less so from the service of their majesties. Some said that I removed my son by withdrawing from the court[160] with their majesties' permission, knowing that the troubles were going to recommence,[161] so I will add a word here. Just as the obscurity of a thick cloud warns us of a coming storm, the maneuvers and the comings and goings of the Cardinal de Lorraine, of the taciturn Spaniard sympathizers among our Politiques,[162] and the massacres, injustices, violations of the Edict and the reform-ers' loss of favor [194] no matter their rank, gave us ample warning of what was to come from this ruptured cloud. And yet I will confess that I did not entirely understand this, nor did I anticipate that we would take up arms again. Indeed I saw the vigilance with which Monsieur le Prince my brother-in-law, the gentle-men of Châtillon,[163] and other seigneurs of the Reformed faith worked to contain so many people, entire cities and regions. These people, subjected as they were to frequent massacres and afforded such meager hope of justice, often felt compelled to make the first move in order to defend their lives, or lose them more honorably, true to their conscience, or to resist murder and torture. However, the prudence of those seigneurs and the rational order that they imposed calmed this agitation, and fueled their hopes as did their majesties with continual promises, vowing and protesting that they desired nothing more than the maintenance of the Edict of Pacification.[164] So that the Edict could be observed, they sent as many letters patent as were requested, but these were nevertheless contradicted by their secret,

160. Jeanne left Paris for her sovereign lands sometime in January 1567. See Albret, *Mémoires et poé-sies*, 45n2, and Roelker, *Queen of Navarre,* 241.

161. A reference to the Second War of Religion which began on September 1567.

162. See Introduction, note 21.

163. "Messieurs de Chastillon" designate the three sons of Louise de Montmorency (1489–1547) and Gaspard de Châtillon (1470–1522). Odet, Cardinal de Châtillon (1517–1571) was the last of the Châtillon brothers to move to the side of Protestantism in 1561; Gaspard, sieur de Coligny (1519–1572), Amiral de France, was one of the principal leaders of the Huguenot resistance; and François, sieur d'Andelot (1521–1569), *Colonel Général de l'Infanterie,* played an important military role in the religious wars until his death.

164. The French royal Edict issued on March 19, 1563 at the château of Amboise and therefore known as the Peace of Amboise. It granted Huguenot nobles the right to hold Protestant services on their estates, but restricted the practice of non-noble French Protestants to a single, designated area outside of urban centers for each baillage (the smallest administrative unit in France). The exceptions to this were cities that Protestants already controlled at the outbreak of the first war where they were al-lowed to maintain their churches, but not add new ones, and Paris and its surrounding area, where no Protestant services were allowed.

sealed letters (we knew about the letters and they made us fear that the intention of their majesties was to overturn the Edict). However, our reverence toward our king, his word, and promises [195] ratified by solemn sermons did not permit us to believe what we saw.

As for the Cardinal de Lorraine, he was not particularly respectful toward the king when he played pelota with the king's faith and honor, and thus made the king contradict himself with his latest Edict and show himself to be deceitful and duplicitous, and provoke the disdain of other kings and foreign princes. Is it then so surprising if the hearts of all his faithful subjects and serviteurs bleed with grief when they see this disgrace reach as high as the king's crown due to the treachery and maliciousness of this wretched and damnable cardinal who abuses his majesty's goodness. We do not in any way believe that the king has in his heart what this impudent monk made him state in the Edict,[165] which everyone knows the cardinal fabricated and sent to the Pope in Rome more than four months ago. Alas! As I said, the hearts of so many faithful subjects bleed, weary of the cardinal's villainy because of the disgrace it brings, dare I say, even to our king? What am I to feel, I who am honored, in addition to the two titles of faithful subject and obedient servant, by that of aunt?[166] In truth I will say that I have never seen, read, or heard anything that angered me and inflamed me so much against the cardinal, and if I came willingly to this cause in good conscience with my son, more willingly still will I continue. Therefore, [196] I am neither acting under duress nor beset by feeblemindedness, as has been said. My righteous anger alone would have sufficed to make me leave my home.

Returning to the subject at hand,[167] hardly had I arrived in my country when rumors of the movement of arms began to disturb all of Guyenne. Those who wrote about the signing by the council of the agreement reached at Marchaiz[168] according to the promise made at Bayonne[169] explain amply why this is so, and I will not comment further. For, having retired to my home, and thinking only

165. This probably refers to the Edict of Saint-Maur, issued by Charles IX on September 23, 1568. This Edict prohibited all religions but Catholicism and ordered the expulsion of Calvinist ministers within fifteen days.

166. Jeanne signed her letters to Charles: "vostre humble et tresobeissante subjecte, et tante, Jane." She was the daughter of Charles's grandfather's (François I) sister (Marguerite de Navarre).

167. Jeanne now goes back in time in order to recount her return to Béarn in late January 1567.

168. The château of Marchais (Aisne) had been bought in 1553 by the Cardinal de Lorraine. In his pro-Protestant recapitulation of all the Protestant accusations leveled at the Guises, François de l'Isle refers, too, to a meeting at Marchais in September 1567 during which the king purportedly accepted to lure Condé and Coligny to Paris to be captured: See François de L'Isle, *La légende de Charles, Cardinal de Lorraine, et de ses frères, de la maison de Guise* (Reims: J. Martin, 1579), 63.

169. A reference to a belief among many Protestants that in 1565 Catherine de' Medici and Charles IX made a promise to the duke of Alva in Bayonne that they would eradicate all Protestant leaders in France.

of my own affairs, I knew only as much of what was happening as was rumored throughout the provinces. I also knew about the strange rebellion in Béarn and later in Navarre[170] of a few of my subjects backed by France (apparent in the letters that their majesties wrote to them). Their internal intrigues, revealed by their own quarrels, led me to anticipate a sad outcome for the affairs of France, but was I certain? No, as God is my witness. This becomes evident with the voyage that I had undertaken to visit my lands, beginning in my County de Foix. When I arrived at Saint Gaudent, a village in Comminges,[171] I met with a gentleman[172] sent by the prince my brother-in-law and Monsieur l'Amiral, who informed me of the taking up of arms and other events well described in [197] what has already been written and need not be repeated here. In my conscience all this seemed so just that I could hold nothing back and offer no less than everything to my God and my king. Even if I had had options at that moment, I would still have encouraged Monsieur de Gramont[173] to take up arms and join the cause with just as much conviction as I did and continue to do.

I returned home with my son to Béarn in order to lead the subjects that God had given me, and prevent, with His grace and every bit of my power, this threatening storm from entering my country. My intention was always to serve my God and my king. I sent one of my men to their majesties to find out what was happening, and to beseech them very humbly to throw water on this fire before it intensified. I remember that in my letter to the queen I used the same or similar words, beseeching her humbly to recognize those who had always been devoted to the service of the crown, and assuring her that she would always find me among those who offered her their faithful service. Furthermore, I would add that I am bewildered about the source of the false rumors that I had sent blank signed orders to their majesties, authorizing the sale of my son's property in order

---

170. A reference to the Catholic rebellions of 1567–1568 in Oloron under the seigneurs Jacques de Sainte Colomme, Gabriel de Béarn, and others, and immediately following in Lower Navarre under Charles de Luxe and Valentin Domesaing. On June 26, 1568, the Catholic rebels surrendered but Charles IX pressured Jeanne to show leniency toward the rebel leaders. See Bordenave, *Histoire de Béarn et Navarre,* 139–50; Roelker, *Queen of Navarre,* 278–79.

171. Saint Gaudens is a commune in the Nébouzan area, not the Comminges area, in Southwestern France (Haute-Garonne).

172. Jeanne's informant has not been identified. According to Bordenave, he would have met her at Saint-Gaudens, two or three days before the Protestant uprising of September 28, 1568, to inform her of it: *Histoire de Béarn et Navarre,* 139.

173. Antoine d'Aure (c. 1526–1576), comte de Gramont and Jeanne's lieutenant général in Béarn and Navarre. He was a moderate Protestant who was respected by Catholics and Protestants. Jeanne may well have needed to persuade him to remain faithful to the Reform cause and reassure herself that Béarn and Navarre would be well defended in her absence. Gramont, in fact, retired to his estates during the Third War of Religion and later abjured his Reformed faith in 1572. This neutrality was rewarded by the governorship of Navarre and Béarn, granted to him in 1572 by Charles IX.

to wage war on the rebels. Certainly, I swear [198] that my property and moreover my life will never be spared against the king's enemies, as has always been the case. But are not the true rebels those who violate the king's ordinances, and those who wish to overthrow his edicts, massacre his people, conspire with foreign countries for their own profit, and seek to exterminate the princes of the blood and faithful officers of the crown in order to execute more freely their evil deeds? Are those actions, in your opinion, intended to preserve the crown entirely for our king? No, no, it is to divide the crown amongst themselves, and throw some morsel of it at the mouths of dogs in order to excite them. It is therefore those rebels that I oppose, and I will continue to offer and indeed put forth my life and possessions in order to punish them. What prevented me from taking a stand in the course of the recent troubles were the rebellions in my lands that were provoked to keep me there. The Sieur de La Mothe Fénelon,[174] sent by their majesties to negotiate my reconciliation with these subjects, knows well whether I hid from him what I had in my heart regarding all that had happened. I kept refuting the words "rebellious" and "seditious" that came frequently from his mouth when speaking of those who had arms in hand for the service of God and the [199] king.[175] I never dissimulated but instead assured him that I was committed, with heart and words, to this cause, whose justice I often debated with him. He countered with arguments so frivolous that there appeared in them more malicious stubbornness than ignorance of the truth. I even went so far as to assure him that, if my son had been able to carry arms, he would have been with the troop of serviteurs faithful to God and their majesties.

During this turbulent time, I communicated constantly, as much with their majesties as with Monsieur le Prince my brother-in-law and his allies, in order to cry "Peace! Peace!" Everyone knows how much I wanted peace, and what joy I felt when a hint of it appeared to us. During the second voyage of La Mothe[176] (who knows that I spoke to him of peace and of my fear that we would fall to where we are now because of the venomous malice of the Cardinal de Lorraine) I uncovered a striking example of the cardinal's malice. They wanted to lure me and my son to court, under the pretense of honoring me and making me the mediator

174. In February 1568 La Mothe was sent by Catherine de' Medici and Charles IX to mediate between the queen of Navarre and her rebellious subjects, although he may have been secretly encouraging the rebels. See Roelker, *Queen of Navarre*, 294; Bryson, *Queen Jeanne*, 169.

175. Here Jeanne refers to the polemic debate over the image of the Protestants after the Tumult of Amboise: were they (according to Catholic propaganda) dangerous political rebels or (according to Protestant propaganda) faithful defenders of the French royal family against the conspiracies of the Spanish-supported Guise faction?

176. In May 1568, La Mothe was sent for a second time to express the king's displeasure regarding Jeanne's treatment of the officers involved in the 1567–1568 uprisings. The real object of his visit may have been to draw Jeanne away from her domains by luring her and her children to court. See Roelker, *Queen of Navarre*, 294–96.

between the king and his subjects of the Reformed faith. La Mothe claimed that peace could not be guaranteed, because the king and queen could not (as he said) be assured of the good will of those of the Reformed faith, and so could not trust them, as would be necessary. [200] Nor, so he claimed, would those subjects have confidence in their king and queen; I alone would have the qualities necessary for those negotiations, for, with regard to their majesties, I had the honor of being in their service and their immediate entourage. Furthermore, according to La Mothe, their majesties had known in me such devotion to their service and to peace in the kingdom that whatever I proposed to them on behalf of those of the Reform would be above all suspicion. On the other hand, I was said to be held in such high regard by those of my faith that they trusted me deeply. Thus, being close to their majesties, and having the opportunity to meet with Monsieur le Prince my brother-in-law and Monsieur l'Amiral, it would be easy for me to alleviate the distrust on one side and the other, and bring together these worthy seigneurs and the king. There you see what sticky sap La Mothe used to coat the sweet words with which he wanted to trap me like a bird. I found those assertions quite strange, even more so the praise he lavished on me regarding my good judgment and prudence. For the discredit and disdain that I had suffered had made me realize that those favorable opinions of me had never actually entered their minds. As for my fidelity and devotion to their service, though their majesties could not possibly have been unaware of them, they always feigned ignorance, as if they had never believed in my loyalty. My response to such a long and florid speech was brief: that I could not believe that anyone [201] wanted to use me in a matter of such great importance, a matter that would challenge the finest minds. La Mothe wanted me to barge in, but I resisted strongly, admonishing him that if I offered to do so without being called upon by them, it would be attributed to audacity on my part, rather than devotion to their service. This caused him to speak even more forcefully; he told me that he had been instructed to speak to me about it. I pressed him to say by whom. He finally told me it was the queen, but that she did not want to be identified. He went on to say that Madame de Savoie,[177] Madame de Ferrare[178] and I had all been suggested, but that the queen had chosen

177. See above, note 141. Marguerite de France maintained close ties with her sister-in-law Catherine de' Medici and important figures at court like Michel de L'Hôpital. She was highly esteemed by humanists, writers, and poets of all factions.

178. Renée de France (1510–1575), daughter of Louis XII and Anne de Bretagne, and sister-in-law to François I, became duchess of Ferrara by her marriage, in 1528, to Ercole d'Este, son of Alfonso d'Este and Lucrezia Borgia. Under her influence, the court of Ferrara became a refuge for those who had taken up the Reformed faith and had fled France, such as Clément Marot. She carried on an extensive correspondence with Calvin until his death. After her husband's death, in 1559, she returned to her French château of Montargis that became a place of welcome for the Protestants. Her daughter Anne remarried the duc de Guise in 1548 and, after his assassination, remarried the duc de Nemours in 1566, thus straining relations between Renée and Jeanne who were opposed in the Rohan affair.

me from among the three (this was an invention to persuade me to undertake the role as mediator, and thus to lure me to court). I replied simply that even if God had graced me with as much skill to conduct this affair as I have devotion to it, I would never negotiate anything at court as long as the Cardinal de Lorraine was there. He responded that once at court, this would be a way for me to get rid of the cardinal.

During that time, La Mothe came to the Basque territories on several occasions to reconcile me with those subjects who had rebelled against me in my kingdom, favoring them in every respect against all reason.[179] Nevertheless, I had promised the king to trust La Mothe in these negotiations; I kept my promise, against my better interests.[180] He was hoping to [202] strike a blow against the Reformed faith, but in that regard he achieved nothing. On his final departure after so many trips, as he was mounting his horse to leave for court, he once again brought up our earlier conversation and entreated me persistently to write to the queen that I would do whatever duty required in order to preserve peace. This was during the time when the Edict of Longjumeau was proclaimed in certain places, like Paris,[181] while being protested in Toulouse and elsewhere.[182] It seemed to me that my offer was not presumptuous, and for that reason I sent to their majesties at Court Vaupilière,[183] one of my men, well informed about the specifics concerning

179. The ostensible object of La Mothe's first visit in February 1568 was to persuade Jeanne to pardon the Navarre rebels. But Jeanne firmly believed that his real assignment was to encourage the rebels. See Roelker, *Queen of Navarre*, 294.

180. Under pressure from the French crown, Jeanne was forced to pardon those who opposed her religious reform and took part in the 1567, 1568, and later the 1569 uprisings. On this question of pardon see Roelker, *Queen of Navarre*, 278–90.

181. The Peace of Longjumeau was signed at Longjumeau on March 23, 1568, and recorded on March 28 by the parlement of Paris.

182. According to Robert J. Knecht, the Peace of Longjumeau "was almost certainly a trap designed to bring about the destruction of the Huguenot leadership.… The course of events that followed [this Edict] suggests a concerted policy of duplicity by the crown aimed at taking the Huguenot leaders by surprise and exterminating them once they had lost their forces." Knecht, *The French Civil Wars, 1562–1598* (Harlow, UK: Pearson, 2000), 143–44. Throughout France, there were many violations of the agreement of Longjumeau. Roelker notes, "In Toulouse, the parlement beheaded the bearer of the king's instructions to proclaim the Edict, disregarding a royal safe-conduct. … The populace forced its way into the parlement of Rouen on the day the peace was registered (causing the parlementaries to flee) prior to killing many Huguenots and destroying their property." *Queen of Navarre*, 292–93. The greatest opposition, however, came from the Catholic leagues and confraternities that formed in the summer of 1568 at Bourges, Orléans, Angers, Troyes and Le Mans in addition to those which had already been set up in Burgundy.

183. Antoine Martel, sieur de la Vaupillière (sometimes written as Vaupilière or Voupillière), was sent by Jeanne to the king with the *Articles envoiez par la Royne Jeanne de Navarre au Roy tant sur l'observation de l'Edit de Pacification que pour le Gouvernement de Guyenne*. See Roelker, *Queen of Navarre*, 296.

the massacres, violations of the Edict, and the machinations of the Cardinal de Lorraine in Toulouse and Bordeaux. He was also to beseech them very humbly if it pleased them to make use of my services in some way, that the cardinal not be present, for my loyalty is incompatible with his disloyalty. As I said in my letters to the queen, if the will of God [203] had been to take her majesty when she was so ill in Meulan, the Cardinal de Lorraine intended to serve Sicilian Vespers[184] to Monsieur le Cardinal my brother-in-law as well as those he thought could spoil his plan to overturn the Edict of Pacification and bring unrest to France.

That attempt thwarted, he tried many others, leaving us where we are now. I wrote to them too about the fear I had that all of this would make us fall back into misfortune. I remonstrated[185] with them in complete humility, as their most humble servant, driven by duty to protect the peace and best interests of this kingdom. I thought of a means that seemed to me not only good, but necessary (since even their majesties complained that their edicts were not obeyed): I proposed that my son, now advanced enough in years, begin his service to their majesties in the government of Guyenne. So that he might be better instructed by the time he came of age, I beseeched their majesties most humbly that they allow him to travel through the principal cities of his lands and enforce observation of the Edict of Pacification, from which Guyenne was profiting little. I hoped to preempt those who, eager as they are to ruin the house of Bourbon rather than see it flourish, and prevent their majesties from honoring my request, could have made the unfounded accusation that my son would crush one party in order to bring relief to the other, since he was of the Reformed faith. For this reason, I beseeched their majesties most humbly to give my son the Sieurs Candale,[186] Marquis de [204] Villars,[187] de Caumont,[188] de Lausun,[189] de Byron,[190] and de Jarnac[191] to accompany

---

184. On "Sicilian Vespers" see above, note 38.

185. This was considered a right of the king's subjects, and it might mean to advise, admonish, reprove, or petition.

186. In order to facilitate the transition of power to her son (he would exercise the positions of governor and lieutenant-général of Guyenne, powers that, in Jeanne's view, Monluc wrongly exercised), she submitted to the king the names of six prominent noblemen of Guyenne who could act as Henri's counsellors: Bryson, *Queen Jeanne,* 175. One of these was Henri de Foix, seigneur de Candale, a Catholic, who married Marie de Montmorency, the daughter of Anne de Montmorency, connétable of France.

187. Honorat de Savoie, marquis de Villars, also a Catholic, succeeded Monluc as lieutenant général of Guyenne in September 1570.

188. On François Nompar de Caumont, see above, note 125.

189. Another member of the Caumont family, not identified with certainty.

190. Armand de Gontaut, Baron de Biron (1524–1592), named maréchal of France in 1577, a Catholic.

191. Guy Chabot, Baron de Jarnac, a Catholic.

and counsel him, having named them intentionally because the majority of them were Roman Catholics.

I thought my request exempt of emotion and partiality, and so just, that a favorable response was a foregone conclusion: *fiat*. I spoke all the more confidently since the grandeur and authority of my son were at the service of their majesties, and since La Mothe had so wanted to persuade me with all his speeches of the favor that I should expect. He all but guaranteed the positive outcome of everything I undertook for my affairs, which he admitted (because he could not deny it) had been neglected, much to his regret. But now that I was to serve in such matters, all efforts would be made to give me satisfaction. This is why in addition to the remonstrance I addressed to their majesties and my offer to strive for the conservation of a just peace, I made the request concerning Guyenne on behalf of my son. But the opinions and changes of the court also changed the favorable response that I should have had, and that was promised to me. For as I previously stated, La Mothe's maneuvers and the promised favors were only to lure me and my son to court.

However, while La Mothe was negotiating this with me, the Cardinal [205] de Lorraine found a quicker strategy which I mention in my letters.[192] His strategy was to send the Sieur de Losses[193] to me with a double mission: one gentle approach and one harsh. Gentle in words, I mean, not in deed, for he was to fill my ears with sweet promises, evoking favor, honor, and profit, in order to lure my son to court. They gave the Sieur de Losses a second mission because they feared that I would see right through their malice, and if I removed the sugar, I would discern the bitterness that it covered, and with that realization, I would make use of similar guile and reply to them with my own sweet words, pledging to send my son but stalling for time. So, the Sieur de Losses was to turn to harsher means and snatch my son from my arms, either by duplicity in the course of a hunt, or by force with the help of Monluc and of some of my own subjects. I was alerted by diverse sources[194] as soon as the Sieur de Losses started his journey, which was halted by the hand of God through a bout of diarrhea, affording me the time to think of my own protection. What made them abandon the use of gentler means and turn to force sooner was that they needed to hurry if they hoped to catch

192. In her letter of September 16, 1568 to Charles IX, Jeanne accused the Cardinal de Lorraine of having ordered the kidnapping of her son: Albret, *Lettres suivies d'une Ample Déclaration*, 198n163.

193. Jean de Baulieu, sieur de Losses, a Catholic. In 1562, when Jeanne was sent away from court, forced to leave her son behind, the sieur de Losses was named by Antoine tutor of Henri to replace Jeanne's Protestant tutors. When, five years after the death of Antoine, Jeanne resumed control of her son's education, Henri's former tutors (Beauvoir and La Gaucherie) were reinstated.

194. On August 12, 1568, Jeanne was informed that the sieur de Losses intended to kidnap her son. See Anne-Marie Cocula, "Été 1568: Jeanne d'Albret sur le chemin de La Rochelle," in Berriot-Salvadore, Philippe Chareyre, and Claudie Martin-Ulrich, *Jeanne d'Albret et sa cour*, 42–43.

everyone at once. The Sieur de Tavanes[195] was charged with surrounding Monsieur le Prince de Condé my brother-in-law in Noyers[196] and Monsieur l'Amiral at Tanlay,[197] while the Sieur de Martigues[198] was charged with surrounding Monsieur d'Andelot[199] in [206] Bretagne.

Voupillieres arrived at court during their deliberations and was retained there for a time, because they believed that before he could get back to me, all would be done. In truth, he brought me a very strange response, far removed from the hope that La Mothe had tried to give me. It would take me too long to describe the language they used and the harshness with which they treated Voupillieres; I will only say that they responded to the just request that I made for my son (as I mentioned earlier) that he was too young to meddle in politics, that he should go to court to accompany the king in his honorable pastimes, and that he should only occupy himself with youthful pursuits. As for the Cardinal de Lorraine, that I should not implore the king to remove him from his private council, for it neither should nor could be done. Moreover, no further action would be taken in response to the detailed instructions that Voupillieres had delivered because he had gone by way of Noyers. They said that my seal had been altered and my instructions had been meant for Monsieur le Prince my brother-in-law in Noyers; I had charged Voupillieres to convey to the Prince his responsibilities regarding my affairs and thank him for the honorable aide he had offered when my subjects from Lower Navarre had risen up against me.

It seemed to me quite [207] harsh and strange to find fault with my friendship and alliance with my brother-in-law, the uncle of my son and the one who

195. Gaspard de Saulx-Tavannes (1509–1573), named lieutenant général of Bourgogne in 1556, member of the king's intimate council in 1563, and maréchal de France in 1570. His role in the affair evoked here remains unclear. Some historians believe that he was given the charge of arresting Condé and Coligny but that he was unwilling to lend himself to such a scheme, others claim that he was the author of the whole plan. See Jouanna et al., *Histoire et dictionnaire*, 1280–81; Henry M. Baird, *History of the Rise of the Huguenots of France* (New York: Charles Scribner's Sons, 1900), 2: 265–67; Cocula, "Été 1568," 42–43; and Roelker, *Queen of Navarre*, 293 and 370n.

196. In July 1568, after the Saint-Valéry episode, Condé entrenched himself in Noyers, a small fortress in Bourgogne that he acquired through his wife. See Haton, *Mémoires* 2:537–39 and Albret, *Mémoires et poésies*, 66n4.

197. Tanlay is within a few miles of Noyers. At the beginning of July 1568, Coligny was staying at the château of Tanlay that belonged to his brother, François de Coligny d'Andelot. See Albret, *Mémoires et poésies*, 67n1.

198. Sébastien de Luxembourg, vicomte de Martigues (d. 1569), colonel général of infantry, appointed lieutenant général, and governor of Bretagne in 1565. During the French Wars of Religion, he fought on the Catholic side.

199. After the siege of Chartres, François de Coligny, seigneur d'Andelot, the Admiral's brother, had retired to his lands in Bretagne. In August 1568, he was in Laval, a town that belonged to his wife, Claude de Rieux. See Albret, *Mémoires et poésies*, 67n3.

took the place of his father (especially since I have always treated Monsieur le Cardinal, my other brother-in-law in exactly the same way). It was all too evident what they had against him, for it was after peace had been negotiated. At the time, their majesties were sending the Prince my brother-in-law the sweetest words of trust, but at court no one hesitated to speak critically and unequivocally since all the prey was thought to be trapped in their nets. This confidence was evidenced by the good cheer that the Cardinal de Lorraine shared with the first Président de Thou.[200] In order to persuade him to provide money, the cardinal confirmed the good news with his customary clapping of hands in moments of joy. But his joys were short-lived as it turned out again.

Not to digress any further, I will say that Voupillieres found me in Nérac,[201] where I had gone, having discovered that the Sieur de Losses was intending to do me this good turn. I thought that if he decided to use force, I would have the best chance of resisting there. We were then visited by our relations, neighbors, and subjects, including Monsieur le Marquis de Villars, Sieur de Caumont and others, to whom I complained about what I knew to be Sieur de Losses's mission, supported, or to be more precise, commanded by the Cardinal de Lorraine. There is scarcely a well-born person who does [208] not know the king to be a gentle and humane prince; such a cruel act—to have an only son wrenched from the arms of his mother—could not have come from him. Moreover, the king's command alone would have sufficed without resorting to force. In obedience, I had traveled as far as Nérac, but with arms being brandished on all sides, I had stopped there to avoid getting caught up in the melee. For, seeing the Catholics arm themselves and hearing them repeatedly brag that in a month there would be no more Huguenots in France, those of the Reformed faith also armed themselves to defend their lives.

So I stayed in Nérac, but not without difficulty. Monluc knows how many times I prevented our people from assembling first;[202] I sent back several who were frightened as much by the news of the Sieur de Losses's attempt to kidnap my son as by the papists'[203] threats. Seeing all of these sinister omens of war and considering the responses forged in the cardinal's back room and brought by Voupillieres, I finally came to the realization, to my great regret, that the kingdom's affairs were

---

200. Christophe de Thou (1508–1582), father of the celebrated historian Jacques Auguste de Thou (1553–1617), first president of the parlement of Paris, Mayor of Paris, chancellor to the duc d'Anjou and the duc d'Alençon, advisor to three kings (Henri II, Charles IX, and Henri III), and a strong advocate of the Catholic party. See Jouanna et al., *Histoire et dictionnaire*, 1328–30.

201. Jeanne would have arrived at Nérac on August 15, 1568: Albret, *Mémoires et poésies*, 70n1.

202. Monluc makes mention of a hundred letters or so that Jeanne would have written to the king to assure him of her desire to maintain peace in her estates: Blaise de Monluc, *Commentaires 1521–1576*, ed. Paul Courteault (Paris: Gallimard, 1964), 636.

203. Disparaging term for Catholics commonly used by sixteenth-century Protestant writers.

on the verge of ruin. Instead of taking good and prompt measures, based on counsel received daily from their most loyal subjects and *serviteurs*, their majesties allowed the enemies of the kingdom to batter its foundation through their crimes [209] and their challenges to the king's very authority in his edicts. The situation worsened so rapidly that I was forced to set aside my own affairs and meditate with my friends and *serviteurs* upon the arrival of all these storms and the consequences they might bring: the revival of past troubles and the great violence that forced those of the Reformed faith to arm and defend themselves. For every one situation that once pushed them to such action, there were now ten.

I reached the following conclusion: one of two things could happen. In order to dam the impetuous river of suffering, their majesties would agree to listen to the advice of their pious subjects (who kept warning them about the harm done to France and suggesting a remedy for it) and would choose to believe them and bring those subjects closer to them. Or their majesties would become hardened by evil and abandon the helm of this poor kingdom to the winds and tides of adversity in the hands of its traitorous pilots, in whom they place too much trust. In that case, it would be absolutely necessary that the princes of the blood (bound as they are by a more personal duty), and following them, the nobility and the people, all as faithful subjects and *serviteurs*, put their shoulders forcefully to the wheel and oppose by all possible means the ruin of the kingdom. [210] The Cardinal de Lorraine would take advantage of the confusion caused by our resistance and would attempt nothing less than to have us all killed. The cardinal's plot has in fact since been unmasked by the letter from Cardinal de Crequy's agent (about which I will say no more as it is printed below). With those intentions, the Cardinal de Lorraine convinced the king to spend huge sums to retain a large number of French and foreign forces, which would otherwise be superfluous in time of peace. I will touch upon this later when I describe what followed.

I foresaw that things could not remain as they were, that either I had to resolve to hold on to the peace that was slipping away from us, as I have said, or to resign myself to war if peace were to fail. I therefore prepared for one and the other. However, desiring to try peace first, I did all I could to prevent the raising of arms in Guyenne whether it be on one side or the other, for I saw our enemies strangely excited and unrestrained in words and deeds, Guyenne, of all the provinces, being the one to benefit least from the peace. All those of the Reformed faith were on the edge of despair because of it, both noble and commoner wandering in the fields, unable to return to their homes; this made it impossible to continue to restrain them. During these two or three weeks that I [211] stayed at Nérac, I did all I could to keep the peace, as my messages and frequent trips to see Monluc confirm. I had sent someone, not long beforehand, to visit Monsieur le Prince my brother-in-law, so as to maintain our friendship (as the honor that I received from the late king his brother dictated that I should), a friendship strengthened, furthermore, by our shared religion. He was as distressed as I was to see France's ills worsen, our enemies arm themselves and rise up on all sides, noblemen massacred in their homes, citizens slaughtered in their cities, and so little justice in response to all of this. He informed me that he had sent their majesties his complaints and warnings[204] (as I had for my part) and he had always received in response expressions of their distress regarding these calamities and their promises of justice as had the Sieur de Teligny[205] in his negotiations with their majesties. Therefore the Prince de Condé and his allies were waiting patiently for these promised outcomes and he entreated me adamantly to keep those of the Religion from taking up arms in Guyenne. This serves to refute those who have said and who write every day that we were the first to take up arms. It is indeed true that we took up arms, but it was to protect our lives from our enemies who were already armed so that we could use our lives and arms in the service of God and of our king.

There I was in that state of anguish, awaiting what should have resulted from those pretty promises. [212] I sent word again to the Seigneurs Prince and Amiral because I had already had wind of the plot to capture them. But the man I sent found them leaving Noyers and Tanlay.[206] They have declared often enough how they left,[207] so it is not necessary to repeat it here. But I would like to say that when my messenger recounted to me the way they departed and their journey across the fields, I felt both joy and sorrow beyond expression—joy at seeing the miraculous deliverance that God by his infinite goodness had granted them, and sorrow at seeing the princes of the blood, such close relatives of my son, wandering thus across France. They were forced to flee the shameful prison and ignominious death that would have followed from the machinations (revealed

---

204. Between April 24 and August 22, 1568, Condé addressed five letters to the king, complaining about the breach of the Edict of Longjumeau. These letters can be found in H. E. P. d'Orléans, duc d'Aumale, *Histoire des princes de Condé pendant les XVIe et XVIIe siècles*, 2: *Pièces et documents* (Paris: Calman Lévy, 1863), 349–58.

205. Charles de Téligny (1535?–1572), the Amiral de Coligny's son-in-law and one of the first victims, with Coligny, in the massacre of the Saint Bartholomew's Day. A sympathizer of the Reformation, he was put in charge of several negotiations, acting as mediator between his party and the French crown. In July 1568 he was entrusted by Coligny with the presentation of a letter of remonstrance to the king. This letter can be found in Jean de Serres's *Mémoires de la troisième guerre civile et des derniers troubles de France* ([Geneva : Meidelbourg], 1571), 36–42. On Téligny see Jouanna et al., *Histoire et dictionnaire*, 1323–25 and Albret, *Mémoires et poésies*, 76n1.

206. Condé and Coligny left Noyers and Tanlay on August 23, 1568: Albret, *Mémoires et poésies*, 77n1.

207. A rare testimony concerning the flight of the princes of the blood in August 1568 is mentioned in Albret, *Mémoires et poésies*, 77n2: *Lettres et remonstrances au Roy par Louis de Bourbon, prince de Condé … avec la protestation dud. s. prince* (Paris, BnF LB 33 n° 238); the text is included in Landré and Martel, *L'Histoire de nostre temps*, 88–100.

clearly enough by their writings) of this Hydra;[208] for every wicked head of his that one cuts off, seven more appear. But, in the end, he[209] will find that God, the just judge, is his Hercules, since he does not believe him to be God. His barbaric cruelty has spared no one, regardless of age or sex. For what constituted this army with which they said that my brother-in-law took to the fields? Carts, coaches and litters—what, full of arms? No, of pregnant women and little children, cradles and nursemaids.[210] The innocent cry of these little creatures was their trumpet call to saddle up. The *fleurs de lys* with which their blood is sown,[211] instead of inspiring reverence and restraining the cardinal's fury [213], intensified his rage. As I mentioned in my letters to the king, this is like ripping off the branches in order to uproot afterward the trunk that is our king;[212] we can no longer ignore it.

I have spoken enough about their voyage; it is time to speak of mine. I saw the cloud that I have described burst and let forth a horrible clap of thunder in the form of the letter from the Cardinal de Crequy's agent and the threat it contained. And, with no evidence for a guaranteed peace, I prepared for a righteous war: the taking up of arms for the legitimate causes of the glory of God which we see every day trampled underfoot, and the blood of his elect spilled. The authority of his majesty was so disdained by these rebels who have broken his edicts and defied his commands that he no longer held the rank of king among them, and the princes of his royal blood were chased by foreign usurpers from the place they should possess. I would like to know how long our subjects can reconcile their resignation[213] to the sights and sounds of such things with fidelity to their God and their king. As for me, I consider those who condone these horrors, either through stupidity or cowardice, no less guilty than those who commit them. For, if we have the means to pull a man from the water and we leave him to drown, are we not murderers? Are we not even more compelled, when we see [214] the

208. In Protestant propaganda, the nine-headed serpent that could grow two new heads for each one cut off, also known in Greek mythology as the Hydra of Lerna, symbolizes the Catholic League and the ever growing evil that it brings along with it. One good example of this association is the representation of Henri IV as Hercules vanquishing the Lernaean Hydra by Toussaint Dubreuil around 1600. As editor of Albret, *Mémoires et poésies*, at 78n1, Ruble sees in this image the expression of the Protestants' hatred for the Cardinal de Lorraine.

209. In French, *Hydra* is a feminine noun, but in her subsequent references to the Hydra, Jeanne uses the masculine singular pronoun *il* (he), underlining the association she is making with the Cardinal de Lorraine.

210. Coligny left with his daughter, the future wife of Teligny, and his young sons, as well as the wife and infant son of his brother d'Andelot. Condé was accompanied by his wife, who was pregnant, and by several children. See Baird, *History of the Rise of the Huguenots*, 2:268–69.

211. A striking image to designate the princes of the blood.

212. See Jeanne's letter to the queen mother, 163.

213. The etymological sense of the French word *pacience* (from the Latin *pati* = to endure, to suffer) is rendered here by the terms *how long* and *resignation*.

obvious danger facing the kingdom with the persecution of the Reformed faith, the crown of our king half on the head of his enemy, to take action and topple the crown since we hold that God has empowered us to avenge such acts? If we had not acted thus, we would have earned, and rightly so, the epithets of traitors, rebels, and subversives, assigned to us by the cardinal and his supporters, who truly hold those titles.

So I resolved to make my way with my children to the home of my brother-in-law, to join my life, wealth, and resources with theirs as I had always been willing to do. I did not want to return to the misery that my son and I suffered during the earlier troubles when we were detained and rendered useless through the malice of some of our subjects. It caused me great distress to see my son, at his age, left behind with the womenfolk. So I took him on this voyage most willingly, for the greatest desire I ever had was that the first time he take up arms would be out of dedication to the glory of his God, the service and defense of his king and country, and the duty to his lineage, which are (as I have amply explained) the three reasons that forced me to leave my country. Do not presume that I undertook this voyage lightly. Know that I did not do so without battling both myself and others. For Satan, who opposes the good and those transformed through God's pure grace into [215] instruments of good, lost no time sleeping when he saw that the saintly zeal of God's glory urged me onward. Satan made use of the powerful to flatter me and make me promises, but to no avail because I was sufficiently accustomed to this sort of trickery and could resist ambition and avarice, vices so unworthy of a noble heart. As he saw that he was wasting his time with this strategy, Satan incited some of my serviteurs against me, serviteurs, I say, of various temperaments, some shamelessly cunning, others worldly-wise, some of them completely ignorant, and still others rashly zealous, and—let's not forget—the fearful. In short, he did not overlook anything that he thought might dissuade me from my Christian endeavor. The most audacious tried to make me doubt the righteousness of the cause, citing reasons that are so commonly known that they need not be restated. But did I need to listen to their reasons any more than a twenty-year-old youth needs the eyeglasses of an old man of sixty? Far from being understandable and convincing, their reasons appeared to me so puny and so muddled that there was nothing as unclear to me as what they claimed to demonstrate. Those who thought to defeat me were defeated and fell into the pit that they had dug for me (where they will remain unless God lifts them out of it). To my deep regret, I must say that they dragged many down with them while I remained firm in my beliefs, principally [216] because of my conscience, guided by the word of God. But in truth, who is so ignorant (whether deliberately, unwittingly, or maliciously) as to resist the compelling arguments written by the most learned men of our time, who depicted in such vivid terms the righteousness of our cause and the legitimacy of our taking up arms. I know some who in their conscience are secretly won over by this cause, and who would confess loud and clear, as we do, if only ambition, greed, or the pursuit of favor had not first taken hold of their hearts.

Oh, you poor wretches who embrace all the prestige and promises, and inflate yourselves with vain hopes! Hold fast to whatever satisfaction you obtain while ignorance lulls you into oblivion, for when truth awakens you, those rewards will vanish like a dream. It will then be too late for you to repent; your grief will last longer than the rewards you expected, regret will march before you, shame will follow on your heels. By the just judgment of God, your conscience will perpetually torture you. You will be despised by both one religion and the other. This is the language I used in speaking to that sort of person, answering evil with good, and commending salvation to them, whereas they wanted to wrest it from me. These reckless fools may have failed, but close behind followed the next battalion, those who value only their own judgment, [217] believing they can thus penetrate the depths of the most secret things in the world. They alleged that it is crucial, indeed essential, that princes maintain peace in their territories. They believed this to be true especially for a small kingdom between larger ones in turmoil and they counseled me to reach out to one side with one hand, and to the other side with my other hand. It was truly like floating between my conscience and the world, favoring the cause while holding on to what was necessary for coexistence with my adversaries. But those wretched fools (I use here the words of the respected author who says that worldly wisdom is folly before God),[214] they wasted their breath, for their words bore no fruit other than a reputation as frauds who, having first fooled themselves, wanted to pull everyone down to their state of folly. Their caution, based on fallacious reasoning, did not triumph over my simplicity, for he who said that he would confound things that are by those that are not,[215] strengthened the frail vessel in me.[216] I made use of the two-edged sword that is the word of God[217] in order to convince those arrogant people who believed that their judgment could contain all the knowledge in the world, and I merely cited the same passage that I used to defend myself against the claim that I had insulted them by calling them fools. That is the passage that states that the wisdom of this world is folly before God, even when we want to relate it to his commandments, [218] trying to render them intelligible, but we cannot reconcile our human capacity to understand with the humble obedience that he requires of us. This humble obedience cannot in any way conform to the wisdom of this

214. The paradox of wisdom and folly can be found in 1 Corinthians 3:19. The author to whom Jeanne refers here may be St. Paul, Desiderius Erasmus (*In Praise of Folly*, ca.1509) or even her mother (*Comédie de Mont-de-Marsan*, ca. 1548).

215. 1 Corinthians 1:28.

216. Wisdom of Solomon 14:1–5.

217. Psalm 149:6.

world. For it is written that he who puts his hand to the plow and looks back is unworthy of the kingdom of heaven.[218] We should not fear an edict that banishes us from the kingdom of France, which is our home for only the very short span of our lives, but instead the irrevocable edict that chases us from the kingdom of heaven for all eternity.

Those who let themselves be carried away by their frivolous imaginations more out of ignorance than malice contrasted the travails ahead of me with the peace at home, which, in their opinion, I could righteously enjoy in good conscience and in accordance with the Reformed faith. I willingly tolerated their ignorance, and I responded more gently to them than to the others that it is not hardship in the name of duty but rather peace too eagerly sought for the sake of convenience that should be called affliction. I added that when we are called by legitimate vocation to serve the glory of our God, all countries must be our home. To speak frankly, I rebuffed rather forcefully the insolent, the worldly, and the ignorant. But let us turn to the rashly zealous, in particular those bound by love of their country, who reproached me [219] that it was not the right thing to leave my lands, for which I was responsible before God, and abandon them in my absence to the threat of plunder by foreigners.[219]

They insisted that charity begins at home, and that this injustice affected my many subjects, not just me and my children. They applied their predictions to the cause to which they saw me so attached, saying that my children and I were public figures, and that we must not put ourselves in such danger. On the one hand, they portrayed so vividly the plight of an afflicted people deprived of the support of their sovereign lady, on the other hand, they spoke of matters of conscience which filled my heart with compassion (I must confess here my weakness), moved as I was by the natural love to which my subjects are entitled.

Finding my resolution shaken, I strove to fortify myself, turning to the wise providence of my God (without which not a single hair can fall from our heads).[220] I concluded that I could not abandon my endeavor, that I ought to leave my lands in his care, and nevertheless make use of all means that he afforded me to delegate in my absence the administration of my lands to trustworthy men.[221] What I used to combat my doubt, I also used to resist the temptation of those rash zealots. I

218. Luke 9:62.

219. Many believed that Philip II of Spain had pretensions toward the Béarn and Lower Navarre. The fact that he offered to intervene for Catherine de' Medici in the affairs of Béarn and Navarre as soon as he learned about Jeanne's flight, and the fact that the queen mother politely declined his offer are signs that these beliefs were not totally unfounded. See *Lettres de Catherine de Médicis*, 3: 188, Letter of September 30, 1568 to Monsieur de Fourquevaulx, French ambassador in Madrid.

220. Matthew 10:30; Luke 12:7.

221. Guy d'Auvillars, seigneur d'Arros, a zealous Protestant, was left in control of Béarn and Navarre when Jeanne left for La Rochelle, replacing the less resolute Antoine d'Aure, comte de Gramont. Later, the governorship was shared with Bernard d'Astarac, baron de Montamat. See Bryson, *Queen Jeanne*,

had not completely recovered from the rude shock I suffered when along came the timid ones. With reasons that appeared obvious in [220] worldly terms, they enumerated the dangers on the roads: the enemies' forces close by while our own forces were scattered here and there; our foes, so cruel and savage that they did not distinguish between the noble and the commoner, sparing no one regardless of rank, age, or sex. Whereas the docility of the rashly zealous moved me to pity, the rigidity on the part of the timid inspired in me an entirely different emotion. The fear of a shameful retreat made me blanch; the danger of a brutal prison made me tremble. Tears came to my eyes at the thought of being separated from my children, and I let myself be persuaded by the timid that I would avoid all that harm by abandoning such a voyage and retreating to my home.

I was nearly defeated and yet felt that I must not be. What, then, did I do? I took the time to plumb the deepest recesses of my conscience, and while thinking about the tranquility that had been presented to me, I recalled, in fact, the worries that I had experienced during the previous conflict. How could I sleep soundly upon learning of the massacre of my brothers? I know that here the brothers of iniquity will mock this word "brothers" (as is their custom), but God will be their judge, as he is mine. To return to the awakening from this sad sleep, what use are all the comforts and beauty of my estates to me, except to remind me of the distress [221] of so many poor souls banished from their own homes, wandering here and there, and reduced to begging for things that they were accustomed to giving to others. My heart froze a thousand times a day, knowing that our people, even my close relations and dear friends, were subject to the infinite dangers that arise during a cruel war. This affliction suffered by the entire Reformed church trickled down to me as a member, in the form of a smaller scale civil war in my sovereign lands. Thus it seemed that God was showing me that those who believed that prudent strategies could keep them beyond the long reach of his hand can say with the psalmist, "Wither shall I go from thy Spirit? or whither shall I flee from thy presence? If I ascend into heaven, thou art there: if I lie down in hell, thou art there. [...] If I say, Yet the darkness shall hide me, even the night shall be light about me. Yea, the darkness hideth not from thee: but the night shineth as the day [...]."[222] I judged by those words that my inaction in this matter was incompatible with the charity that compels us to help everyone, even servants of the Reformed faith. Indeed, it seemed to me that it was not enough to pity them, but that I had to roll up my sleeves and take action.

What bothered my conscience even more was seeing my son old enough, if not to take up arms, at least to begin his necessary military training. I will tell you that this concern did not leave me a moment's reprieve until I took him where

176 and 238 ; and Mlle Vauvilliers, *Histoire de Jeanne d'Albret: Reine de Navarre*, 3 vols. (Paris: L. Janet and F. Guitel, 1818), 2:313.

222. Psalm 139:7–8; 11–12.

he is now,[223] by the grace of God. While debating thus with myself, not only did I have to combat foreign adversaries, I was also at war [222] with my own instincts. My own will turned against me. My flesh assailed me and my spirit came to my defense. If one hour I felt better, the next I felt worse. In short (because these emotions are difficult to describe and can only be judged through experience), I implore those who have been there, and whose hearts have been tried like gold in a furnace,[224] to take the time to imagine my torment, rather than reading about it. Believe that our ancient enemy Satan, who by his long experience learned these arts more perfectly than any man, did not forget solemn rhetoric, persuasive eloquence, honeyed flattery, nor gilded lies as means to achieve his ends. He knew well how to choose his own instruments to accomplish those ends. Sensing his instruments too weak against me, he went as far as to tempt my soul, and won over half of my will to combat the other half. Nevertheless, in the end I emerged victorious by the grace of my God.

I spend too long on this point, and I believe that I have explained well enough the battles I endured to remain steadfast in my earlier resolution to undertake my voyage. I wanted to explain this in detail in order to anticipate the allegations and close the mouths of those who would accuse me of rushing, eyes closed, into the cause, like the ill-advised writer who composed an aggravating little pamphlet entitled *Response à un certain escrit publié par l'Ad-*[223]*miral et ses adherans* [A response to a certain publication by the Admiral and his followers].[225] The author, ill-informed regarding my disposition and that of my son, says in one passage that the Amiral, taking advantage of the feeblemindedness of a woman and a young prince who holds the honor of being first in line to the throne after the king and his brothers, tricked them into joining his coterie, against the advice and wishes of their closest relations, friends, and serviteurs, and of the majority of their subjects. He further claims that the Amiral beguiled them into recklessly taking up and sharpening arms, turning those arms against themselves, and endangering what remains of their lands in order to seek, along with their own ruin, the ruin of the king, his people, and all the princes, seigneurs, and gentlemen of this kingdom.[226]

I decided to include, word for word as it is written, the passage that concerns my son and me in order to respond to it. Although they did not quite dare mention us specifically by name out of fear of being shamed for these impudent lies, they nonetheless let everyone know precisely whom they meant by using

223. That is to say under the military supervision of Condé.

224. Proverbs 17:3.

225. Antoine Fleury, *Responce à un certain escrit, publié par l'Admiral et ses adherans, pretendans couvrir et excuser la rupture qu'ils ont faite de l'Edict de Pacification* (Paris: Claude Fremy, 1568), was a refutation of a remontrance sent to the King by Coligny. Coligny deplored the calamities that occurred in France since the second edict of pacification.

226. See Fleury, *Response à un certain escrit*, B, recto and verso.

indirect references. As for the words "feeblemindedness of a woman and a child tricked by the Amiral," they should have searched for something more clever to say, since they meant to defame him and scorn us, than that we were called to a cause, something we demonstrated [224] by the fervor with which we embraced that cause long ago and most willingly (without need for force or trickery).

What I have written above will be sufficient proof of the stupidity of this fabricated lie. I will not waste my time with this scornful epithet of feminine feeblemindedness, for if I wished to undertake here the defense of my sex, I have enough reasons and examples against this bighearted man (who speaks of women almost out of pity) to demonstrate to him that he has misused the term in this context. I will now turn to the youth who is so close to me that, though truth inspires my argument today, I will always be accused by the mean-spirited of being swayed by maternal affection. It will suffice to say (for people today are quick to understand) that if he were still feebleminded at the age of fifteen he would hold little promise for the future, which (thank God) nobody believes. By suggesting this, they denounce the education he received at the feet of his king in his majesty's private council (a school to turn the most ill-mannered into refined and honorable gentlemen). He was not tricked into the cause due to any imbecility; rather it pleased God to grace his heart with zeal. God's glory, the service of his king (for he is not such a child that he does not know his duty), and the friendship for his close relatives are the three ties that attached him to the cause.

As for the passage where this author honors my son by referring to the rank of first prince of the blood, after the king and his brothers, judge for yourself [225] his intended malice from what follows. In order to make the lies that he tells about my son afterward seem more distasteful, he starts with this white background the better to accentuate the blackness he adds later. He begins by saying that we came lightly to our decision [to leave our lands], which makes us, in his opinion, unforgivable. The difficulties that I described above respond sufficiently to that accusation. He then adds "against the advice and will of their closest relations, friends, serviteurs and vassals. I am astonished at these blind fools who want to judge appearances, and persuade themselves of things that do not exist, or if they do exist, they do not really support the argument as this author claims. Recognize that all of our relations, friends, serviteurs, and subjects are divided into three camps: one group belonging to the Reformed church, another belonging to the Roman Catholic Church, and the rest who are part of a third order, who blow both hot and cold, and whose advice cannot be considered reliable. I will leave it at that, and I believe that everyone realizes that my relatives who are dedicated to the same cause as I also share my opinions. Concerning the others, they are our adversaries in this, and consequently cannot be believed. And I can attest that they did not make it difficult for us to counter them, for they hardly came forth with any arguments. I think that he who wrote that little book would have had us believe that the sieurs de Guise, in particular the cardinal, were close to my son. But what brute ignorance! Does anyone believe that we are such imbeciles, my son and I, that [226] the memory of the initial hardships that they inflicted on the late king my husband, and that they have since continued to wreak on our house, did not teach us to be wary of them, they who opposed our very honor, lives, and estates? Truly, I declare that if we had trusted their advice, we would have rightly earned the title of imbeciles.

As for my serviteurs, the number of faithful and good ones has been large enough, thanks be to God, to have fortified my Christian fervor with their opinions and counsel. I have also had some bad serviteurs as I mentioned above. Although they attempted to ruin me through demands for honorific medallions, estates, and favors, they only gained what I was willing to lose. Concerning my vassals, the majority of them from Guyenne (where almost all of our holdings are located), are they not the ones who accompanied us here? As for the Navarrois and Béarnais, I do not count as loyal subjects those who were seduced and led away with letters and handsome promises made by the very people who are behind that aggravating little pamphlet. Those subjects who are loyal are from both religions and in greater number than may be thought. Some are taking up arms with my son; the others have remained in our lands, committed to our service, loyally opposing campaigns that my enemies want to undertake there. Clearly that ignorant writer expressed what he wishes were the reality rather than what is. Especially when he speaks of what we [227] did against the will of our relations, friends, serviteurs and subjects, he does not accuse us of some minor infraction, for he claims that we took up arms, sharpened them, and turned them against ourselves. As I said in my letter to the queen of England,[227] he claims that we pointed these arms against the heavens and the king; God forbid that such impiety and disloyalty should have ever come near the hearts of those of Bourbon and Navarre.

Furthermore, what he accuses us of doing is the opposite of what we actually did, which was to take up arms for the service of our God, king and country (this is so often said, written, and believed by good people, princes, and foreigners that it would be superfluous to repeat it here). He adds that we put in obvious peril what lands remain to us. Since he speaks of the remaining lands, this would mean that the kingdom used to be intact.[228] Everyone knows this and knows that the breaking up of the lands was in the service of the crown for which we do not hesitate to risk the rest. However, we would not do so, nor would we risk our own ruin (as he claims) by pursuing the ruin of the king, the people, the princes, and the gentlemen of this kingdom. If the author and his supporters can see beyond the ends of their noses, let them recognize their own guilt. Among so many persuasive

227. See above, 48–49.

228. The kingdom was intact before the conquest, in 1512, of the Southern part of the kingdom (Upper Navarre) by Ferdinand of Aragon.

examples, I will content myself with choosing [228] one in response to each accusation (such examples can be found in several texts and the subject of my book provides enough arguments without inflating my writings further). Regarding the king, I refer them to the book that was written in favor of assigning the crown of France[229] to the Guises. Regarding the people, I point to the massacres of Vassy,[230] of Meaux, and too many others.[231] Regarding the princes, I cite the conspiracies to deprive the late king my husband of his rights, the imprisonment of Monsieur the Prince his brother at Orléans[232] and the very recent attempt to hunt him down.[233] Regarding the gentlemen, they tried by all possible means to exterminate so many nobles and great captains (who can be more accurately counted now that they are assembled into an army than when they were dispersed). By weakening the forces of the king, they made it easier to diminish his authority, which they have already so seriously undermined. They would have accomplished that long ago if not for the staunch opposition of the good and loyal subjects and serviteurs of his majesty, princes, gentlemen, and people, whose number is so great that if my son and I had not already been united by that same devotion, we now would not dare raise our eyes to heaven.

If the Cardinal de Lorraine and his followers believe that they can smother our truths with their plan to spread their repulsive and absurd lies in writing, let them peddle their silly tales elsewhere. If his brazen maliciousness has not

---

229. A reference to the 1559–1560 controversy about King François II's young age. Various Protestant pamphlets, such as the *Légitime conseil des Rois de France pendant leur jeune aage, contre ceux qui veulent maintenir l'illegitime gouvernement de ceux de Guise, sous le titre de Majorité du roi*, claimed the regency for the king of Navarre since François II was still a minor. In response, Jean du Tillet, *greffier* of the parlement of Paris, published *Pour la majorité du Roy très-chrestien, contre les escrits des rebelles* (Paris: Guillaume Morel, 1560). Because Tillet traces the Guises' genealogy back to Charlemagne, some thought that this tract had been written in support of the Guises' pretensions to the French crown. See Albret, *Mémoires et poésies*, 99n1. Many of these Protestant pamphlets have been reproduced in the *Mémoires de Condé, servant d'éclaircissement et de preuves à l'histoire de M. De Thou, contenant ce qui s'est passé de plus mémorable en Europe* (London: chez Claude du Bosc & Guillaume Darrés and Paris: chez Rollin, fils, 1743) 1:433–70.

230. On March 1, 1562, François, second duc de Guise, traveling to his estates, stopped in Vassy where he came across a large congregation of Huguenots worshiping outside the prescribed limits. Events rapidly escalated, and fire was set to the barn where the worshipers had assembled, wounding and killing a large number of unarmed Huguenots. This incident, often minimized by Catholics and interpreted as premeditated murder by Huguenots, sparked the First War of Religion.

231. The "Surprise of Meaux," a failed conspiracy organized by Condé on September 28, 1567, triggered new outbreaks of violence and the Second War of Religion. See Jouanna et al., *Histoire et dictionnaire*, 1385–88. See also note 25.

232. A reference to the Amboise Conspiracy, also known as "Tumult of Amboise," and Condé's subsequent arrest on October 30, 1560, under the Guises' suspicion.

233. A reference to the failed attempt to arrest Condé at Noyers in the fall of 1568, supposedly planned by the Cardinal de Guise.

chased all shame from his heart, he should now blush, recognizing the failure of his primary goal which was to render us and our actions loathsome, [229] both among foreigners and in our own nation. By the great goodness and providence of our God, they are forced to see their conspiracies, councils, and campaigns being overturned, foreigners from all sides offering aid to the cause, driven by their zeal for God's glory, old friends of the crown bringing support, the French hurrying from all provinces and assembling like a colony of ants, joined together miraculously to ratify with their lives and possessions the loyalty sworn to their king under the first Princes of his blood. I want people to examine impartially the miraculous way in which this Christian army, loyal to its God and its king, came together from the four corners of the kingdom, despite the promise made to their majesties by the governors of the provinces to prevent even four armed Huguenots from coming together in one place without their being carved into pieces.

Credible witnesses have written about the dangers that Monsieur le Prince my brother-in-law and Monsieur l'Amiral escaped during their voyage, the previously unknown places they found to cross the river,[234] the favor that Monsieur d'Andelot received from the heavenly father as he crossed the Loire,[235] which (following the example of the Red Sea)[236] provided a path to the children of God. They have also written of the shame that accompanied the end of the Sieur de Martigues's campaign.[237] [230] Whereas those who crossed the river make the woods and the plains resound with psalms and thanksgiving (not to vaunt their

234. The bridges and the fords were guarded, but an unguarded ford was discovered not far from the city of Sancerre, by which, on a sandy bottom, the fugitives were able to cross the Loire. See Agrippa d'Aubigné, *Histoire universelle*, book 5, ch. 4, ed. André Thierry (Geneva: Droz, 1985), 3:24–30.

235. The drought that so reduced the stream as to render the passage practicable was regarded by the Protestants as a sign of Providence, as well as the sudden rise of the river, immediately afterward, which baffled their pursuers. See Baird, *History of the Rise of the Huguenots*, 2:269–70 and Bryson, *Queen Jeanne*, 179–80.

236. A reference to Exodus 15:21–27. The flight of Condé, Coligny, and their followers from hostile Catholic France is compared to the flight of the People of Israel from their bondage in Egypt. Both signal a double miracle: the drought allowing the crossing of the river Loire on foot and horseback, which is reminiscent of the withdrawal of the waters of the Red Sea, and the sudden rise of the river, immediately afterward, preventing the Catholic troops to pursue the fugitives as the return of the waters had covered the host of Pharaoh. On the Loire crossing as a sign of Providence see Baird, *History of the Rise of the Huguenots*, 2:269–70; on the Red Sea analogy see Bryson, *Queen Jeanne*, 177–88. According to Protestant historians, Protestants would have crossed the Loire river singing the translation of Psalm 114, *In exitu Israël*: see Albret, *Mémoires et poésies*, 103n3.

237. A reference to the so-called "Combat de la Levée" on the banks of the river Loire, between Angers and Saumur. It opposed the Protestant troops led by d'Andelot, Montgomery, La Noue, and others to Martigues's Catholic garrison, small but including veteran soldiers and excellent musketeers. Martigues was later joined by Montpensier. François de La Noue, who was a participant, recounts this incident in his *Discours politiques et militaires*, ed. F. E. Sutcliffe (Geneva: Droz, 1967), Discours XXVI, 712–17. See also Aubigné, *Histoire universelle*, 3:18–23.

glory, but to celebrate the goodness of the great God of hosts), we will be silent, my son and I, about having seen the hands of the adversary bound, and his courage so shaken that we could say: "The stouthearted are spoiled: they have slept their sleep and all the men of strength have not found their hands."[238]

Three or four days before my departure from Nérac, did Monluc, knowing that some men were assembled at the port of Tonneins to protect the passage that most of those from Guyenne would have to cross, not declare that he would hack them to pieces if they did not leave? Likewise, he said that if those of the county of Armagnac assembled, and others of the duchy of Albret, not a single one would escape. Truly, according to what the eyes of this world can judge, it was hard to believe what we saw. For (as I said) Monluc, as a veteran warrior, had foreseen all this and had given orders in Guyenne, and also in Agen, Lectore, and Condom, such that there was not a river passage nor a bridge that was not seized and kept under guard. Moreover, he had approximately sixteen companies of soldiers, all of them prepared [231] to march at the sound of a whistle. As regards his infantry, he established thirty new *commissions* in addition to those already in place, and all this within ten leagues of him. So who could have thought that the unfortunate faithful would have been able to congregate? In those areas there are so many papists that no one can so much as leave his house without it being known. Who would have ever believed that my son and I could escape surreptitiously and extricate ourselves from all the troops surrounding us? Whoever we are, let us admit that no man knew of a way out.

All the same, this did not prevent my son and me from leaving, for we were certain that our God, under whose guidance we placed ourselves, knew well by what path to lead us for his glory. On Friday, September 3, 1568, I received word[239] that Monsieur le Prince my brother-in-law (as I have amply described) had left his home in great haste. I was informed of the route he took and the limited number of men he had with him, who had, in fact, joined him along the way. I sent one of my men to Monluc the following Saturday and apprised him of the arrival of my brother-in-law and the wrong that had been done to him; I informed Monluc of everything that had happened. On Sunday, September 5, we celebrated Holy Communion at Nérac, imploring the good Lord's aid [232] through public and private prayers. On Monday,[240] we left Nérac accompanied by only fifty gentlemen out of all the domestic serviteurs and subjects who were with us, and went to

---

238. Jeanne cites the very popular French translation of Psalm 76 by Théodore de Bèze. The translation given here from the Geneva Bible differs in style.

239. François de Bricquemault, a Protestant and advisor to Jeanne d'Albret, was the messenger. On October 27, 1572, he was publicly hanged on the Place de Grève in Paris for alleged complicity in Coligny's conspiracy against the king. He protested to the last that he had neither taken part in, nor heard of any plot against the king or the state.

240. Monluc thought that Jeanne left on Sunday. See Monluc, *Commentaires*, 637.

spend the night at Casteljaloux, one of my cities and principal estates. I notified Monluc,[241] who informed me that he was going to Villeneuve d'Agen to assemble his captains in order to attend to the situation in Guyenne.

That is how I managed to leave in the open and with his knowledge, not three leagues away from him. The seventh day,[242] I stayed at Casteljaloux, because my niece, Mademoiselle de Nevers,[243] was ill, not having fully recovered from the smallpox that she suffered at Nérac. Her fever returned, so I sent her back to Nérac with some of my women, and I left the following day, Wednesday the eighth. I went to Tonneins, where I spent Thursday and Friday. The Sieur de La Mothe arrived at Tonneins, sent to me by their majesties, and brought me letters from them, informing me that my brother-in-law had been taken prisoner, and that Monsieur l'Amiral was with him. Their majesties complained that Monsieur le Prince and l'Amiral had taken up arms against them, and commended me to their majesties' service. I thus realized that they had been fed the lies of the Cardinal de Lorraine and his supporters. Because the Sieur de La Mothe saw that I was so far along on my voyage (which surprised him greatly), in my opinion he did not tell me everything that he was supposed to. For, either [233] out of fear or swayed by his conscience, he could not respond to the reasons I gave for having come this far. He even admitted (as I said in my letter to the queen) that my intentions were good, and consequently he did not dare denounce in my presence the intentions of Monsieur le Prince my brother-in-law, nor those of the *seigneurs* who were with him. But he would have liked to persuade me that they would have been welcome at court, and that by setting down their arms they would have obtained everything they wanted. Such promises so often made, and just as often broken, helped me thrust aside these distractions. I promised La Mothe that I would endeavor to negotiate a just peace, but things were so bitter on both sides, and one side (that is the Cardinal de Lorraine) was so entrenched in its malice that I was still waiting to use my good will to fulfill my duty, whenever God in his goodness would present me with a means to do so. I believe that La Mothe did not hide from their majesties our discussions, during which I made every effort to explain to him the sincerity of our service to them, our grievances, the destruction brought to France by these troubles, the circumstances that had given birth to and fed these troubles,

241. Jeanne sent one of her servants to Monluc's castle at Estillac to inform him of her departure for Casteljaloux, and express her regrets to Monluc's wife, Françoise de Tilladet, who was supposed to visit Jeanne with her children and Monsieur de Sainct-Orens. See Monluc, *Commentaires*, 637 and Bryson, *Queen Jeanne*, 189–90.

242. September 7, 1568.

243. Marie de Clèves (1553–1574), last child of the duc de Nevers and of Marguerite de Bourbon-Vendôme, who was the elder sister of Antoine de Bourbon. Marie was brought up by Jeanne d'Albret as a Calvinist. She was married to her first cousin, Henri I de Condé. The couple abjured their Protestant faith in 1572 after the Saint Bartholomew's Day Massacre. In 1574, Henri fled the court and converted back to Protestantism. Marie stayed behind and remained Catholic.

and the means to eradicate them. He consistently responded that he found my words [234] good and true, assuring me that he would relay them to the king and queen, which I believe he did.

So you see how those who manipulated their majesties used a contemptible ploy when they made them send a letter patent to the court of parlement of Toulouse to seize our property in Guyenne,[244] and send a commission to the Baron de Luxe[245] for my sovereign lands. All this was done under the guise of charity and for the supposed protection of our property because, according to them, my son and I are prisoners. La Mothe could have testified to the contrary, if he wanted to, and all the more so if he remembered my son's response to the first harangue he addressed to him when La Mothe arrived and asked my son why he had left our home and was getting involved in the troubles. My son answered him with the quick wit typical of his age and his region that it was to spare expenses for mourning clothes, because if the princes of the blood were killed one after the other, the surviving one would have to mourn the first one whereas if they died together, neither of them would need mourning apparel.[246] That was why he was going off to find Monsieur his uncle, in order to live and die alongside him. I think that La Mothe delivered his impromptu harangue because he believed my son so young and foolish that he was there without knowing why. The following day, my son let him know, in no uncertain terms, that he knew well who was the spark and the torch who set France ablaze. [235] For hearing La Mothe inveigh against this fire, he told him that he would attempt to put it out with a pail of water. Unsure of what he meant, La Mothe asked him how he would do that. He answered, "By making the Cardinal de Lorraine drink until he bursts." I recount these two stories about my son not to boast about him, nor to act as his historiographer, but rather to let everyone know that he did not come to this cause as a child led by his mother, but that his own innate will was joined with mine because he recognized the excellence of that cause, which is to say the service to God, the king, and his kinsmen.

244. A reference to Charles IX's letters patent of October 15 and November 19, 1568, confiscating all of Jeanne's holdings. See Albret, *Mémoires et poésies*, 112n2 and Bryson, *Queen Jeanne*, 207.

245. Charles de Luxe, eldest son of Jean IV de Luxe and Isabeau de Gramont, was a member of a well established family in Navarre; he also enjoyed the protection and favor of the King Charles IX (Chevalier de l'ordre du roi, promoted in 1566 lieutenant for the king of France in the viscounty of Soule and governor of the château of Mauléon). In 1567 he led the revolt of the people against Jeanne in Basse-Navarre and the viscounty of Soule. In 1568 Charles IX gave him authority over Jeanne's lands. See Kevin Gould, *Catholic Activism in Southwest France, 1540–1570* (Aldershot, UK: Ashgate, 2006), 152–53.

246. It was customary for the king, at the death of his close relatives, to provide his followers (princes, lords, officers, and courtiers) with mourning attire. See Albret, *Mémoires et poésies*, 114n1.

I stayed at Tonneins on Friday to wait for my sénéchal of Armagnac, Fonterailles,[247] who was bringing with him most of the nobility by horseback, and his brother, the Sieur de Mont-Amat,[248] who was leading the infantry. This gave Monluc all the time in the world to come arrest me, which he tried to do, hastening to assemble his forces, which he had readied at Villeneuve d'Agenois by Sunday the twelfth. The preceding Saturday,[249] I left Tonneins where I had received word from Monsieur le Prince my brother-in-law, who was at Saintes with Monsieur l'Amiral, and I spent the night at La Sauvetat. The following day I went to Bergerac, where I found most of the nobility of Périgord ready and willing to sacrifice life and possessions to the general cause, which seemed to greatly surprise [236] La Mothe, because included among them were gentlemen of the highest rank. Between La Sauvetat and Bergerac, those who were in the château d'Eymet fired several arquebuses and killed some of our infantrymen as they passed.[250] This forced our infantrymen to fight back and storm the château in the presence of La Mothe who, upon seeing these few men in action, realized that they were not a motley crew (as is so often reported to their majesties), but steadfast and valiant troops.

I kept La Mothe at Bergerac Monday, Tuesday, and Wednesday, while I wrote letters, which he was to deliver to Monsieur le Prince my brother-in-law, to their majesties, to Monsieur brother of the king, and to Monsieur le Cardinal, my brother-in-law. Anyone can read these letters in print,[251] but because they seemed to me too brief, I decided to declare clearly my purpose by writing this expanded treatise.

Thursday the sixteenth, I departed for Mussidan, and along the way I encountered the Sieur de Bricquemault,[252] whom Monsieur le Prince my brother-in-law was sending to me to assume command of our troops under my son's

247. Michel d'Astarac (after 1535–after 1610), baron de Marestaing et de Fontarailles, second son of Jean-Jacques d'Astarac and Anne de Narbonne, colonel de la cavalerie de Jeanne d'Albret, appointed sénéchal d'Armagnac in 1565, fierce defender of the Protestant cause. In his *Commentaires*, 596–99, Monluc recounts how he took the château of Lectoure in September 1567.

248. Bernard d'Astarac, baron de Montamat or Montmaur, brother of Michel, governor and lieutenant général de Jeanne d'Albret's Protestant army, a highly respected captain. Pierre de Bourdeille, seigneur de Brantôme, highly praises his bravery: Brantôme, *Discours sur les colonels de l'infanterie de France*, ed. Étienne Vaucheret, preface by V.-L. Saulnier (Paris: Vrin, 1973), 119. After accompanying Jeanne to La Rochelle in 1568, Montamat joined Mongommery and fought by his side in 1569, and later conquered the entire Bigorre region.

249. Saturday, September 11, 1568.

250. Monluc makes no mention of this incident; see his *Commentaires*, 637–38.

251. It is from Bergerac, where Jeanne sojourned until September 16, that are dated the first four letters reproduced here. See 2–19.

252. See above, note 239.

authority. It amazes me that the brave Capitaine d'Escars[253] did not come closer to see us, given that he had written to their majesties (as La Mothe reported to me) that he had four thousand gentlemen under his command in Limousin and Périgord to prevent even a [237] single Huguenot from budging. But what he meant, in my opinion, was four thousand pigs, which in his village are called gentlemen, because they are dressed up in silk. We traversed the passages that he had endeavored to guard, and rather than advancing toward us, he fled.[254] In a letter that he wrote to the Capitaine, Monluc tried to bolster his courage, but this is a quality d'Escars never had in his heart, and has not yet embraced.

After a day in Mussidan, we stayed Saturday and Sunday in Aubeterre,[255] and then Monday, Tuesday, and Wednesday in Barbezieux. We spent Thursday in Archiac, where we learned that Monsieur le Prince my brother-in-law was headed towards us. He stopped at Cognac, because the inhabitants took rather a long time to open the gates. We went to find him in the countryside, my son and I, and I could not say who was happier: he to see us, or we to have found him. For my part, it seemed that finding him was the culmination of my mission, which God through his divine grace had so well guided through to the end. Here, I delivered my son into the hands of Monsieur his uncle, so that under his guidance and the tutelage of his wisdom and valor, my son would fulfill the vocation to which God had called him: once he had acquired experience and means, he would be able to devote them as well as his life to the service of his God, king, and lineage. It was for these three reasons that I placed him [238] in the hands of Monsieur his uncle, and sent him to the Christian army. Those who only think of me as a mother, and therefore as a woman, and my son as a child raised at my side with love and tenderness, will suppose that many tears were shed at our parting, because of our closeness, my sex, and his age. However, in order to demonstrate to everyone with what devotion I dedicated him to such an excellent cause, and with what enthusiasm he went, I will say that joy shone in our eyes and illuminated both our faces. The gladness of leaving each other for such a purpose overcame all the obstacles presented by age, sex, and blood ties. I recommended him to this great God, and secondly to Monsieur le Prince, my brother-in-law. He departed; I remained at La Rochelle,[256] deprived of domestic comforts, and yet utterly content to endure this for my God.

253. Capitaine de gendarmes (1565–1578), governor of Bordeaux, see above, note 93. Jeanne's animosity may be explained by the fact that he had been a treacherous servant of Antoine.

254. Jeanne's perception of this event differs from Catherine de' Medici's: see *Lettres de Catherine de Médicis*, 3:188, Letter of September 28, 1568, to François d'Escars.

255. September 18 and 19, 1568.

256. On September 28, 1568, Jeanne d'Albret arrived at La Rochelle with her son. They were received with acclaim. See Bryson, *Queen Jeanne*, 204.

I beseech those who read this to excuse the style of a woman who considered the subject of her book so worthy that it did not require beguiling words to embellish it, only the truth which she so faithfully observed. Although she may be called ignorant and feebleminded, she will at least be called truthful.

1559

The first national synod meets in Paris and produces the *Discipline*, a document that establishes the governance and structure for the French Reformed Churches.

King Henri II dies after a jousting accident. He is succeeded by his fifteen-year-old son, François.

1560

A Huguenot conspiracy to take control of King François and the queen mother Catherine de' Medici at Amboise fails. Louis de Condé is implicated in the plot, arrested and condemned to death.

King François II dies and is succeeded by his ten-year-old brother, Charles. Catherine de' Medici becomes regent during her son's minority, outmaneuvering Antoine de Bourbon, first prince of the blood.

Louis de Condé is liberated and later declared innocent by the parlement of Paris.

Jeanne d'Albret openly espouses the Reformed faith.

1561

François de Guise, Anne de Montmorency, and Albon de Saint-André form the Catholic "Triumvirate" to defend the Catholic faith in France confronted with what they deem to be the royal family's unacceptable tolerance of Huguenot nobles.

Pope Pius IV reconvenes the Council of Trent, an ecumenical council that meets to reform Catholic practices and define Protestant heresy.

Catherine de' Medici holds the Colloquy of Poissy, a meeting that assembles Catholic clergy and theologians and Protestant ministers to seek common religious ground. The meeting ends in failure.

1562

King Charles IX orders parlements to register the January Edict. This royal edict recognizes the freedom of conscience in religious matters, but outlaws Reformed services in towns.

François de Guise and his men kill Huguenot worshippers whom they find holding a service in the town of Vassy (Wassy). The incident becomes known as the Massacre of Vassy.

Several Huguenot uprisings trigger the First War of Religion.

Louis de Condé takes the city of Orléans.

Antoine de Bourbon dies of wounds received in the battle of Rouen.

1563
François de Guise is assassinated. The Amiral Coligny is suspected by the Guise family of having given the order.

The Edict of Pacification of Amboise ends the First War of Religion. Huguenots' rights of worship are extended to the outskirts of one town per *baillage* and to towns controlled by Huguenots at the end of the war.

Jean-Raymond Merlin is sent from Geneva to help Jeanne establish a Calvinist state in Béarn and Navarre.

Pope Pius IV threatens to excommunicate Jeanne d'Albret.

1564
Charles IX, now reigning in his own name, begins a tour of his kingdom.

John Calvin dies. He is succeeded in Geneva by Théodore de Bèze.

1565
Charles IX and the queen mother meet with the duke of Alba in Bayonne. Protestants speculate that France and Spain agree to assassinate Protestant leaders in each of their countries.

1566
Iconoclastic violence marks the beginning of a Protestant revolt in the Netherlands.

1567
The duke of Alba leads Spanish troops along the eastern French border towards the Netherlands in view of repressing the Protestant revolt against Philip II of Spain.

Louis de Condé leads a failed mission to kidnap Charles IX and the queen mother at Meaux. He and the Amiral Coligny decide to attack Paris and thereby incite the Second War of Religion.

A revolt against Jeanne d'Albret is attempted in Béarn.

1568
Nobles in Navarre revolt against Jeanne d'Albret. Jeanne defeats and pardons the rebel leaders.

The Edict of Longjumeau brings a temporary truce in March.

Chancellor Michel de L'Hôpital, a leader of the moderate Politique party, is dismissed.

Louis de Condé, Amiral Coligny, and Jeanne d'Albret seek refuge in La Rochelle. The Third War of Religion begins in September.

1569
Louis de Condé is killed after the battle of Jarnac.

The parlement of Paris sentences Amiral Coligny to death in his absence.

1570
Jeanne d'Albret helps negotiate the Peace of Saint Germain and the Third War of Religion comes to a close.

1571
The symbolic Cross of Gastines is taken down in Paris. This gesture provokes violent outburst of anti-Protestant violence among Catholic crowds.

1572
Amiral Coligny returns to court.

Jeanne d'Albret dies on June 9.

Jeanne's son Henri de Navarre marries Marguerite de Valois, sister to King Charles IX on August 18.

The Saint Bartholomew's Day Massacre starts on August 24. Thousands of Huguenots, both Parisian residents and nobleman in Paris for the wedding, are murdered.

The genealogical tables that follow include only the names of family members who survived childhood. The names in bold indicate people whom Jeanne mentions in her letters and/or the *Ample Declaration*. In addition to their names, titles are included for these people to aid readers in identifying them within the body of the text.

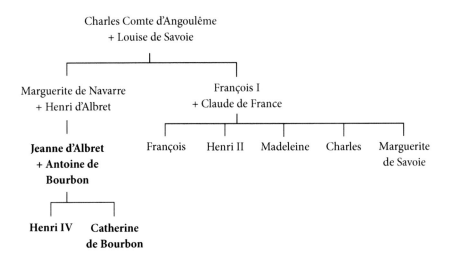

1. Jeanne d'Albret's Family

2. The French Royal Family

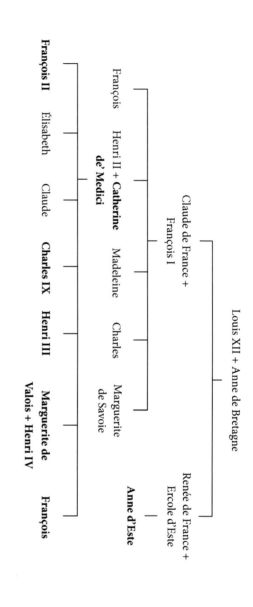

3. The Bourbon Family

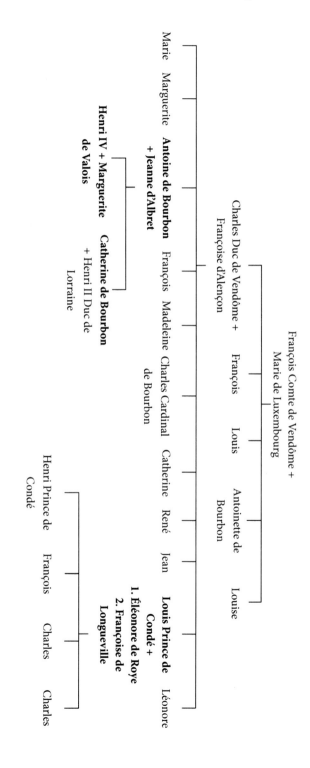

4. The Guise Family

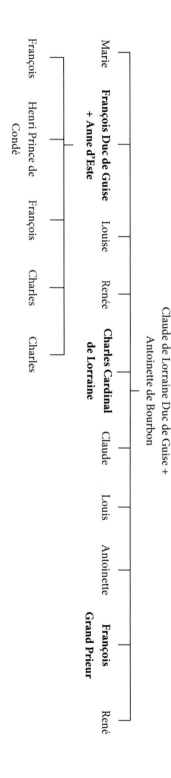

Claude de Lorraine Duc de Guise +
Antoinette de Bourbon

Marie

**François Duc de Guise
+ Anne d'Este**

Louise

Renée

**Charles Cardinal
de Lorraine**

Claude

Louis

Antoinette

**François
Grand Prieur**

René

François

Henri Prince de
Condé

François

Charles

Charles

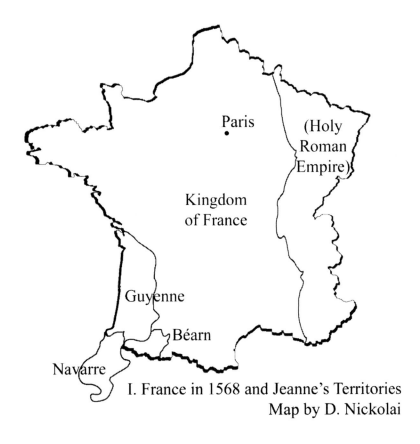

I. France in 1568 and Jeanne's Territories
Map by D. Nickolai

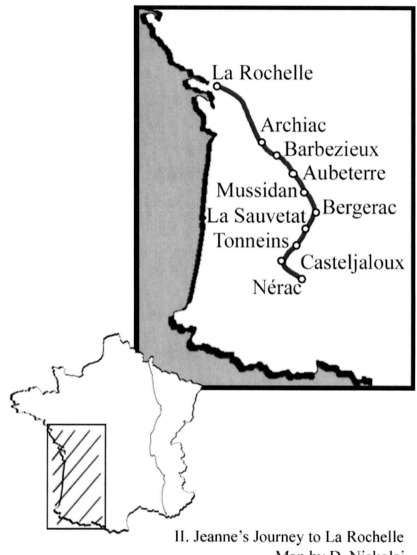

II. Jeanne's Journey to La Rochelle
Map by D. Nickolai

Bibliography

Primary Sources

Albret, Jeanne d'. *Jeanne III d'Albret: Chronique, 1528–1572*. Edited by Bernard Berdou d'Aas. Anglet: Atlantica, 2002.

_____. *Lettres: suivies d'une Ample Déclaration*. Edited by Bernard Berdou d'Aas. Biarritz: Atlantica, 2007.

_____. *Lettres et Ample Declaration des lettres precedentes*. In *L'histoire de nostre temps, contenant un recueil des choses memorables passées et publiées pour le faict de la religion et estat de la France depuis l'edict de pacification du 23 jour de mars, jusqu'au present*. Edited by Christophe Landré and Charles Martel, 160–238. La Rochelle: [Barthelemy Berton], 1570.

_____. *Mémoires et poésies*. Edited by Alphonse Ruble. Paris: Libraires de la Bibliothèque Nationale, 1893. Reprint, Geneva: Slatkine, 1970.

Aubigné, Agrippa d'. *Histoire universelle*. Edited by André Thierry. Vol. 3, *Livres V et VI*. Geneva: Droz, 1985.

Bourbon, Antoine de. *Lettres d'Antoine de Bourbon et de Jehanne d'Albret*. Edited by Mis de Rochambeau. Paris: Renouard, 1877.

Bourbon, Louis I de. *Lettres et remonstrances au Roy … par Louis de Bourbon, prince de Condé … avec la protestation dud. s. prince*. S.l., 1569.

Brantôme, Pierre de Bourdeille, seigneur de. *Discours sur les colonels de l'infanterie de France*. Edited by Étienne Vaucheret, with a preface by V.-L. Saulnier. Paris: Vrin, 1973.

Condé, Louis, prince de. *Mémoires de Condé, servant d'éclaircissement et de preuves à l'histoire de M. De Thou, contenant ce qui s'est passé de plus mémorable en Europe*. London: chez Claude du Bosc & Guillaume Darrés, 1743.

Estienne, Henri. *L'introduction au traité de la conformité des merveilles anciennes avec les modernes ou, Traité preparatif à l'Apologie pour Hérodote*. Edited by Bénédicte Boudou. Geneva: Droz. 2007.

Fleury, Antoine. *Responce à un certain escrit, publié par l'Admiral et ses adherans, pretendans couvrir et excuser la rupture qu'ils ont faite de l'Edict de Pacification*. Paris: Claude Fremy, 1568.

Haton, Claude. *Mémoires de Claude Haton contenant le récit des événements accomplis de 1553 à 1582, principalement dans la Champagne et la Brie*. Published by Félix Bourquelot. 2 vols. Paris: Imprimerie impériale, 1857.

Isle, François de l' (pseud. of Louis Régnier de la Planche). *La légende de Charles, Cardinal de Lorraine, et de ses frères, de la maison de Guise*. Reims: J. Martin, 1579.

La Noue, François de. *Discours politiques et militaires.* Edited by F. E. Sutcliffe. Geneva: Droz, 1967.

Marot, Clément, and Théodore de Bèze. *Les Psaumes en vers français avec leurs mélodies.* Facsimile reprint of Geneva: Michael Blanchier, 1562. Edited and with introduction by Pierre Pidoux. Geneva: Droz, 1986.

Médicis, Catherine de. *Lettres de Catherine de Médicis.* Edited by Hector de la Ferrière-Percy et al. 11 vols. Paris: Imprimerie nationale, 1880–1943.

Monluc, Blaise de. *Commentaires 1521–1576.* Edited by Paul Courteault. Paris: Gallimard, 1964.

Montaigne, Michel de. *Essais.* In *Œuvres complètes.* Edited by Albert Thibaudet and Maurice Rat, 3–1097. Paris: Gallimard, 1962. Reprint, 1976.

Montaigne, Michel de. *The Essays of Michel de Montaigne.* Edited and translated by M. A. Screech. London: Allen Lane, 1991.

Montenay, Georgette de. *Emblemes ou devises chrestiennes.* Lyon: Jean Marcorelle, 1571. Reprint, Menston, UK: Scolar Press, 1973.

Navarre, Marguerite de. *The Heptameron.* Translated by Paul A. Chilton. London. Penguin Book, 1984.

_____. In *Théâtre de femmes de l'ancien régime.* Vol.1: *XVIe siècle.* Edited by Catherine Masson and Nancy Erickson Bouzrara, 35–374. Saint Étienne: Publications de l'Université de Saint Étienne, 2006.

Serres, Jean de. *Mémoires de la troisième guerre civile et des derniers troubles de France.* [Geneva: Meidelbourg], 1571.

Tillet, Jean de. *Pour la majorité du Roy très-chrestien, contre les escrits des rebelles.* Paris: Guillaume Morel, 1560.

Secondary Sources

Aumale, Henri Eugène Philippe d'Orléans, duc d'. *Histoire des princes de Condé pendant les XVIe et XVIIe siècles.* 7 vols. Paris: Calman Lévy, 1863–1896.

Bainton, Roland H. *Women of the Reformation in France and England.* Minneapolis, MN: Augsburg Publishing House, 1973.

Baird, Henry M. *History of the Rise of the Huguenots of France.* 2 vols. New York: Charles Scribner's Sons, 1879. Reprinted frequently.

Barker, Sara K. *Protestantism, Poetry and Protest: The Vernacular Writings of Antoine de Chandieu, c. 1534–1591.* Aldershot, UK: Ashgate, 2009.

Berriot-Salvadore, Évelyne. *Les femmes dans la société française de la Renaissance.* Geneva: Droz, 1990.

Berriot-Salvadore, Évelyne, Philippe Chareyre, and Claudie Martin-Ulrich, eds. *Jeanne d'Albret et sa cour: Actes du colloque international de Pau 17–19 mai 2001.* Paris: Honoré Champion, 2004.

Bordenave, Nicolas de. *Histoire de Béarn et Navarre: 1517 à 1572*. Edited by Paul Raymond. Paris: Mme Veuve Jules Renouard, 1873.

Bryson, David. *Queen Jeanne and the Promised Land: Dynasty, Homeland, Religion and Violence in Sixteenth-Century France*. Leiden: Brill, 1999.

Cazauran, Nicole. "Boaistuau et Gruget éditeurs de *l'Heptaméron*: À chacun sa part." *Travaux de littérature* 14 (2001), 149–69.

Cholakian, Patricia F. and Rouben C. Cholakian. *Marguerite de Navarre: Mother of the Renaissance*. New York: Columbia University Press, 2006.

Cocula, Anne-Marie. "Été 1568: Jeanne d'Albret sur le chemin de La Rochelle." In Berriot-Salvadore, Philippe Chareyre, and Martin-Ulrich, *Jeanne d'Albret et sa cour*, 33–57.

Couchman, Jane. "What is 'Personal' about Sixteenth-Century French Women's Personal Writings?" *Atlantis* 19, no. 1 (1993): 16–22.

Crawford, Katherine. *Perilous Performances: Gender and Regency in Early Modern France*. Cambridge, MA: Harvard University Press, 2004.

Davis, Natalie Zemon. "The Rites of Violence: Religious Riot in Sixteenth-Century France." *Past & Present* 59, no. 1 (1973): 51–91.

Daybell, James. "'I wold whyshe my doings myght be … secret': Privacy and the Social Practices of Reading Women's Letters in Sixteenth-Century England." In *Women's Letters Across Europe, 1400–1700*. Edited by Jane Couchman and Ann Crabb, 143–61. Aldershot, UK: Ashgate, 2005.

Dictionnaire du moyen français: La Renaissance. Edited by Julien G. Algirdas and Teresa M. Keane. Paris: Larousse, 1992.

DMF: Dictionnaire du Moyen Français, version 2012 (DMF 2012). ATILF-CNRS & Université de Lorraine.

Diefendorf, Barbara B. *Beneath the Cross: Catholics and Huguenots in Sixteenth-Century Paris*. New York: Oxford University Press, 1991.

——————. "The Religious Wars in France." In *A Companion to the Reformation World*. Edited by R. Po-chia Hsia, 150–68. Malden, MA: Blackwell, 2004.

Droz, Eugénie. "Antoine Vincent: La propagande protestante par le Psaultier." In *Aspects de la propagande religieuse*. Edited by Gabrielle Berthoud et al., 276–93. Geneva: Droz, 1957.

——————. *Barthélemy Berton, 1563–1573*. Geneva: Droz, 1960.

Ekman, Mary C. "Self-Representation in d'Albret's *Ample Déclaration*." In *The Rule of Women in Early Modern Europe*. Edited by Anne J. Cruz and Mihoko Suzuki, 30–42. Urbana: University of Illinois Press, 2009.

Eurich, S. Amanda. *The Economics of Power: The Private Finances of the House of Foix-Navarre-Albret during the Religious Wars*. Kirksville, MO: Sixteenth Century Journal Publishers, 1994.

Garrisson, Janine. *A History of Sixteenth-Century France, 1483–1598: Renaissance, Reformation, and Rebellion*. Translated by Richard Rex. New York: St. Martin's Press, 1995.

Gould, Kevin. *Catholic Activism in Southwest France, 1540–1570*. Aldershot, UK: Ashgate, 2006.

Graham, Victor E. and W. McAllister Johnson. *The Royal Tour of France by Charles IX and Catherine de Medici: Festivals and Entries, 1564–1566*. Toronto: Toronto University Press, 1979.

Greengrass, Mark. *The French Reformation*. Oxford: Basil Blackwell, 1987.

Guilleminot, Geneviève. "La polémique en 1561: Les règles du jeu." In *Le pamphlet en France au XVIᵉ siècle*, 47–58. Paris: École normale supérieure de jeunes filles, 1983.

Hampton, Timothy. "Examples, Stories, and Subjects in *Don Quixote* and the *Heptameron*." *Journal of the History of Ideas* 59, no. 4 (1998): 597–611.

Harding, Robert. "The Mobilization of Confraternities against the Reformation in France." *Sixteenth Century Journal* 11, no. 1 (1980): 85–107.

Higman, Francis M. *The Style of John Calvin in his French Polemical Treatises*. Oxford: Oxford University Press, 1967.

Holt, Mack P. *The French Wars of Religion, 1562–1629*. Cambridge: Cambridge University Press, 1995.

Jouanna, Arlette, Jacqueline Boucher, Dominique Biloghi, and Guy Le Thiec. *Histoire et dictionnaire des guerres de religion*. Paris: R. Laffont, 1998.

Kettering, Sharon. "Clientage during the French Wars of Religion." *The Sixteenth Century Journal* 20, no. 2 (1989): 221–39.

_____. "Patronage and Kinship in Early Modern France." *French Historical Studies* 16, no. 2 (1989): 408–35.

_____. "The Patronage Power of Early Modern French Noblewomen." *The Historical Journal* 32, no. 4 (1989): 817–41.

King, Margaret L. *How Mothers Shaped Successful Sons and Created World History: The School of Infancy*. Lewiston, NY: The Edwin Mellen Press, 2014.

Kingdon, Robert M. *Geneva and the Consolidation of the French Protestant Movement, 1564–1572: A Contribution to the History of Congregationalism, Presbyterianism, and Calvinist Resistance Theory*. Madison: University of Wisconsin Press, 1967.

Knecht, R. J. *The French Civil Wars, 1562–1598*. Harlow, UK: Pearson, 2000.

Kuperty-Tsur, Nadine. *Se dire à la Renaissance: Les mémoires au XVIᵉ siècle*. Paris: J. Vrin, 1997.

_____. "Jeanne d'Albret ou la persuasion par la passion." In Berriot-Salvadore, Philippe Chareyre, and Martin-Ulrich, *Jeanne d'Albret et sa cour*, 259–80.

_____. "Justice historique et écriture mémorialiste." In *Écriture de soi et argumentation: Rhétorique et modèles de l'autoreprésentation: Actes du colloque de l'Université de Tel-Aviv, 3–5 mai 1998*. Edited by Nadine Kuperty-Tsur, 47–64. Caen: Presses universitaires de Caen, 2000.

Lhuillier, Théophile. *L'ancien château royal de Montceaux en Brie*. Paris: E. Plon, Nourrit et Cie, 1885.

Lyons, John D. *Exemplum: The Rhetoric of Example in Early Modern France and Italy*. Princeton: Princeton University Press, 1989.

Major, J. Russell. "Noble Income, Inflation, and the Wars of Religion in France." *American Historical Review* 86, no. 1 (1981): 21–48.

_____. "Vertical Ties through Time." *French Historical Studies* 17, no. 4 (1992): 863–71.

Matheson, Peter. *The Rhetoric of Reformation*. Edinburgh: T&T Clark, 1998.

Mathieu-Castellani, Gisèle. *La conversation conteuse: Les Nouvelles de Marguerite de Navarre*. Paris: Presses universitaires de France, 1992.

McIlvenna, Una. "Word Versus Honor: The Case of Françoise de Rohan vs. Jacques de Savoie." *Journal of Early Modern History* 16, no. 4–5 (2012): 315–34.

Neuschel, Kristen B. *Word of Honor: Interpreting Noble Culture in Sixteenth-Century France*. Ithaca: Cornell University Press, 1989.

Pascal, Eugénie. "*Lettres de la Royne de Navarre* ... avec une *Ample Declaration d'icelles*: autoportrait d'une femme d'exception." In Berriot-Salvadore, Chareyre, and Martin-Ulrich, *Jeanne d'Albret et sa cour*, 243–58.

Pettegree, Andrew. *The Book in the Renaissance*. New Haven: Yale University Press, 2010.

Pollman, Judith. "Countering the Reformation in France and the Netherlands: Clerical Leadership and Catholic Violence, 1560–1585." *Past & Present* 190, no. 1 (2006): 83–120.

Racaut, Luc. *Hatred in Print: Catholic Propaganda and Protestant Identity during the French Wars of Religion*. Aldershot, UK: Ashgate, 2002.

Ramm, Ben. "Barking up the Wrong Tree? The Significance of the *Chienet* in Old French Romance." *Parergon* 22, no. 1 (2005): 47–69.

Roelker, Nancy Lyman. "The Appeal of Calvinism to French Noblewomen in the Sixteenth Century." *Journal of Interdisciplinary History* 2, no. 4 (1972): 391–418.

_____. *Queen of Navarre, Jeanne d'Albret, 1528–1572*. Cambridge, MA: Belknap Press of Harvard University Press, 1968.

Roussel, Bernard. "Jeanne d'Albret et 'ses' théologiens." In Berriot-Salvadore, Philippe Chareyre, and Martin-Ulrich, *Jeanne d'Albret et sa cour*, 13–31.

Ruble, Alphonse, baron de. *Antoine de Bourbon et Jeanne d'Albret, suite de "Le mariage de Jeanne d'Albret."* 4 vols. Paris: A. Labitte, 1881–1886.

Simonin, Michel. "Notes sur Pierre Boaistuau." *Bibliothèque d'Humanisme et Renaissance* 38 (1976): 323–33.

Stierle, Karlheinz. "Three Moments in the Crisis of Exemplarity: Boccaccio-Petrarch, Montaigne, and Cervantes." *Journal of the History of Ideas* 59, no. 4 (1998): 583–95.

Stjerna, Kirsi I. *Women and the Reformation.* Malden, MA: Blackwell, 2009.

Sutherland, Nicola M. *Princes, Politics and Religion, 1547–1589.* London: Hambledon Press, 1984.

Tulchin, Allan. *That Men Would Praise the Lord: The Triumph of Protestantism in Nîmes, 1530–1570.* Oxford: Oxford University Press, 2010.

Vauvilliers, Mlle. *Histoire de Jeanne d'Albret: Reine de Navarre.* 3 vols. Paris: L. Janet and F. Guitel, 1818.

Vester, Matthew A. *Jacques de Savoie-Nemours: L'apanage du Genevois au cœur de la puissance dynastique savoyarde au XVIᵉ siècle.* Translated from the English by Éléonore Mazel. Geneva: Droz, 2008.

Wiesner-Hanks, Merry. "Protestant Movements." In *The Ashgate Research Companion to Women and Gender in Early Modern Europe.* Edited by Allyson M. Poska, Jane Couchman, and Katherine A. McIver, 129–48. Aldershot, UK: Ashgate, 2013.

Wolfe, Michael. "Bourbon Family and Dynasty." In *Encyclopedia of the Renaissance.* Edited by Paul F. Grendler, 1:265–70. New York: Charles Scribner's Sons, 1999.

Index

Stierle, Karlheinz, 26n
Stjerna, Kirsi I., 4&n
storm imagery, 45, 67, 77, 79
storytelling, 19–26, 53–55, 62–64, 91
Surprise de Meaux, 7
Sutherland, Nicola M., 51n, 64n

Taillevis, Raphael de, 56n
Téligny, Charles de, 78&n, 79n
Thou, Christophe de, 65&n, 76&n
Thou, Jacques Auguste de, 76n
Tilladet, Françoise de, 90n
Tournon, François de, 56&n, 57
Triumvirate, 8&n, 53n
Tulchin, Allan, 11n
Tumult (or Conspiracy) of Amboise,
    7&n, 27

Valois, Elisabeth, 64n
Valois, Marguerite de, 13, 31, 40n,
    60&n
Vaupillière (or Vaupilière). *See* Martel,
    Antoine
Vauvilliers, Mlle., 82n
Vester, Matthew A., 65n
Vigneulles, Philippe de, 20
Voupillieres. *See* Martel, Antoine

wars of religion, 5, 14, 26, 34–35;
    First War of Religion, 5&n, 7, 10;
    Second War of Religion, 5&n, 9,
    43&n; Third War of Religion, 5&n,
    9, 13, 35
Wiesner-Hanks, Merry, 4n
women's writing, 34–35, 50, 86, 93